GOD KNOWS

When Your Worries and Whys Need More than Temporary Relief

Lisa Whittle

W PUBLISHING GROUP

AN IMPRINT OF THOMAS NELSON

God Knows

Published in Nashville, Tennessee, by W Publishing, an imprint of Thomas Nelson.

Thomas Nelson titles may be purchased in bulk for educational, business, fundraising, or sales promotional use. For information, please email SpecialMarkets@ThomasNelson.com.

Unless otherwise indicated, Scripture quotations are taken from The Holy Bible, New International Version®, NIV®. Copyright © 1973, 1978, 1984, 2011 by Biblica, Inc.® Used by permission of Zondervan. All rights reserved worldwide. www.zondervan.com. The "NIV" and "New International Version" are trademarks registered in the United States Patent and Trademark Office by Biblica, Inc.®

Scripture quotations marked CEV are taken from the Contemporary English Version. Copyright © 1991, 1992, 1995 by American Bible Society. Used by permission.

Scripture quotations marked CSB® are taken from the Christian Standard Bible®, Copyright © 2017 by Holman Bible Publishers. Used by permission. Christian Standard Bible® and CSB®, are federally registered trademarks of Holman Bible Publishers.

Scripture quotations marked ESV are taken from the ESV® Bible (The Holy Bible, English Standard Version®). Copyright © 2001 by Crossway, a publishing ministry of Good News Publishers. Used by permission. All rights reserved.

Scripture quotations marked THE MESSAGE are taken from THE MESSAGE. Copyright © 1993, 2002, 2018 by Eugene H. Peterson. Used by permission of NavPress. All rights reserved. Represented by Tyndale House Publishers, a Division of Tyndale House Ministries.

Scripture quotations marked NASB are taken from the New American Standard Bible® (NASB). Copyright © 1960, 1962, 1963, 1968, 1971, 1972, 1973, 1975, 1977, 1995 by The Lockman Foundation. Used by permission. www.Lockman.org

Scripture quotations marked NKJV are taken from the New King James Version®. Copyright © 1982 by Thomas Nelson. Used by permission. All rights reserved.

Scripture quotations marked NLT are taken from the Holy Bible, New Living Translation. © 1996, 2004, 2015 by Tyndale House Foundation. Used by permission of Tyndale House Ministries, Carol Stream, IL 60188. All rights reserved.

Any internet addresses, phone numbers, or company or product information printed in this book are offered as a resource and are not intended in any way to be or to imply an endorsement by Thomas Nelson, nor does Thomas Nelson vouch for the existence, content, or services of these sites, phone numbers, companies, or products beyond the life of this book.

ISBN 978-0-7852-9024-7 (audiobook)
ISBN 978-0-7852-9023-0 (eBook)
ISBN 978-0-7852-9018-6 (TP)

Library of Congress Control Number: 2022944346

Printed in the United States of America

23 24 25 26 27 LBC 5 4 3 2 1

For my daughter Shae and to every other person reading this,
only God knows everything about . . .

Just breathe. He's on it.

Contents

Contents

Introduction

How *God Knows* Can Help You

In a sea of book options and with the looming stack of "to-be-read" books on your bedside table, I can think of three reasons you might have felt compelled to pick up *God Knows*.

1. You're in pain and want relief.
2. You're afraid and want reassurance.
3. You're desperate for hope and, at this point, aren't picky about how you get it.

In each of these instances, you must believe on some level that God can provide those things for you because you've been drawn to the idea that He knows what's happening in *the* world and in *your* world. Good news: you aren't wrong.

God does know. Besides the proof through otherwise-impossible timing, acts of providence, and what people like to call "God winks," we have proof from many places in the Bible. I particularly love how the NIV version of the Bible says it in 1 John 3:20, so simply: "God is greater than our hearts, and he knows everything."

> There's not one thing you did yesterday, face today, or will go through tomorrow that God doesn't know about.

There's not one thing you did yesterday, face today, or will go through tomorrow that God doesn't know about.

That statement could be the end of it if we didn't take issue with our struggle. We have questions, and God is good with them. We may not get the answers we want, but asking means we are interested.

Why, God?

Don't You see, God?

Will You help, God?

Can't You understand how this hurts, God?

At some point, we will want to understand what it really means for us, day to day, that God knows about our lives. If we break this down further, here are our main questions.

How can God knowing help me in what I'm going through?

Our own history with knowledge has proven it inadequate to solve the world's problems. It's helpful with good decision-making and becoming better people, perhaps, but information is unable to change terrible news, prevent sadness or sickness, or drive us into productivity. I've known plenty of people who were knowledgeable and who suffered—brilliant but stuck. If we are using ourselves as the measuring stick, it is no wonder we would assume less of God's all-knowing. But God's knowledge is not on our level, so we are dealing with a different set of rules.

Maybe you've never considered His omniscience important as you drive through Starbucks every day for your hit of liquid energy, but you couldn't be more wrong. You being at Starbucks is under the umbrella of how the God of the universe has intimate knowledge of you, even in your regular life. "You discern my going out and my lying down; you are familiar with all my ways. Before a word is on my tongue you, LORD, know it completely" (Psalm 139:3–4).

How does God's knowledge alone change anything?

Where our knowledge requires additional steps to be effective, God's knowledge is, itself, an action. It is complete—an entire sovereign system. Because it involves no parameter or limit, there is no process required to find out more information or meet more criteria to help. The whole picture is tied into a permanent and supernatural character trait of a perfect and limitless God, not a limited measurement tied to a shifting, imperfect human decision-maker, prone to bias and error (a.k.a., you and me). "As the heavens are higher than the earth, so are my ways higher than your ways and my thoughts than your thoughts" (Isaiah 55:9).

In comparing our knowledge to God's, may we see the critical distinctions and be more eager than ever to surrender our attempts to self-manage. God's omniscience is a system of perfection. It has no gaps. It is not a nebulous concept. His knowing what is going on in our world *is* Him working on our behalf. Those two things cannot be separated. When we understand that, we see how God's knowledge is crucial in our day-to-day lives.

While God's omniscience is not completely definable by human minds like ours, it is important to dive into it, because right now we need some relief and security. When we understand "He's got the whole world in his hands" is more than a slogan or a mirror cling, we can sleep better at night.

And He has been gracious enough to tell us some things about Himself that we *can* understand. The Bible tells us He is pure, unbiased, always aware, trustworthy, thorough, lasting, redemptive, and—maybe most important on many days to our tender hearts—fully *for us*. "The LORD God is a sun and shield; the LORD bestows favor and honor; no good thing does he withhold from those whose walk is blameless" (Psalm 84:11).

Our sun and shield. Favor and honor. That is enough to hang our futures on. No matter how I feel some days, I certainly feel much more solid believing in a God like this than banking it all on empty positive vibes.

There is more to God's knowledge than what I listed, of course. It's important to understand the omniscience of God is not just facts to know about Him; His omniscience is facets of His nature that translate into our daily sustaining. His

> No matter how I feel some days, I certainly feel much more solid believing in a God like this than banking it all on empty positive vibes.

all-knowing is for our well-being. I'm awed that God can be so good to us to share Himself for our benefit. And I'm grateful.

Because life is hard, we might think: *He sure doesn't* feel *good all the time.* Things don't go well all the time, absolutely. If God knows everything, then why would He allow bad things? Why do we experience the constant tinge of worry? Why do we spend so much time fighting for injustices that seem to continue and having no answers when difficulties happen to us? Shouldn't we feel more secure?

There are some reasons we don't feel more secure, comforted, and relieved, even though we might know that God is in control. Hold on to your hat because I write bluntly.

1. **We are doubters.** We can't see God working so we have a hard time believing He has things under control.
2. **We are impatient.** We want things fixed, solved, and vindicated on our timetable.
3. **We are controlling.** We want things done our way, all the time.
4. **We are selfish.** We want a perfect life, no problems, and things skewed in our favor.
5. **We want to be God ourselves.** This is a hard one to swallow, so we generally overlook it. In some ways, it's a combination of all the above, but it goes deeper. Stick with me because this is crucial.

Do you wish you had the power to make everything right in the world, to undo, redo, fix, or solve things, or make everything hard go away by your abilities? We might not come right out and say we wish we could be God, but it is something nearly every person who has ever lived has wanted to do. We've all been looking for a way to escape the basic realities of being a human since God breathed his *rûaḥ* (spirit) into us and we became *nepeš* (a living soul).[1] "Then the LORD God formed a man from the dust of the ground and breathed into his nostrils the breath of life, and the man became a living being" (Genesis 2:7).

Adam didn't *become* God in that moment, of course, nor did we, in the human lineage. Adam *breathed in* God—rather, God breathed his life into him to fill his otherwise lifeless, dust-formed body and bones. Without His breath we wouldn't have existed. And in it, we were intended to begin a lifetime relationship of *reliance*. Without His breath now, we cease to be. He could have breathed Himself into Adam and made him and all the rest of us His clones. But instead, He wanted to make us humans, *given life but dependent upon His*. God intended that we would rely upon Him for our very breath—until we breathe our last and enter into His physical presence where we will need human breath no more. Until then, He promised to provide all we need—wisdom and understanding, strength when we are weak, presence in our lack and loneliness. It was and is a perfect scenario. We just don't like the reliance part.

Yes, our quest for reliance has proven to be an enormous battle, and desiring knowledge is the place we have historically been the most tempted to challenge God. Why? Because Satan has long been luring us there. His goal to get us to self-destruct in pride and control is an easier sell in the innocent packaging of the "good thing" of knowing more. Genesis 2 and 3 prove this point. As chapter 2 introduces us to the scene ("The LORD God took the man and put him in the Garden of Eden to work it and take care of it. And the LORD God commanded the man, 'You are free to eat from any tree in the garden'" vv. 15–16), Genesis 3 shows us the manifestation of the temptation:

> Now the serpent was more crafty than any of the wild animals the Lord God had made. He said to the woman, "Did God really say, 'You must not eat from any tree in the garden'?"
>
> The woman said to the serpent, "We may eat fruit from the trees in the garden, but God did say, 'You must not eat fruit from the tree that is in the middle of the garden, and you must not touch it, or you will die.'"
>
> "You will not certainly die," the serpent said to the woman. "For God knows that when you eat from it your eyes will be opened, and you will be like God, knowing good and evil."
>
> When the woman saw that the fruit of the tree was good for food and pleasing to the eye, and also desirable for gaining wisdom, she took some and ate it. She also gave some to her husband, who was with her, and he ate it. (vv. 1–6)

We want to know when we don't understand. We want to control when things are not controllable. We struggle with reliance. We want to do God's job. But we aren't very good at it. We've proven that.

I'm not here to try to work miracles in the next eight chapters. I can't work a miracle in your life anyway. What I hope to do, instead, is give some insight and tools to get us at least closer to being

> We want to know when we don't understand. We want to control when things are not controllable. We struggle with reliance. We want to do God's job.

people who gain their hope and strength from deferring to God. I am praying that you walk away from this book feeling like the words *God knows* mean something far deeper than a saying you might wear on a shirt. I hope you start to say them when your world is caving in around you. My prayer is that you will have found a new way to breathe in and out life—a new way of coping, a new perspective and level of trust in more than yourself.

For the Do-It-Yourselfers

You might be glad to know that in this book, I am offering one "to-do," but it may not be in the way you usually think about it. Since learning more about ourselves hasn't improved our angst but has, in many ways, increased it (self-discovery brings unending to-do lists), we will take a breather from our search to know ourselves better and instead get to know more about God. Learning about the nature of Christ changes the way we function as people. The more we trust in His omniscience, the more we will rest in a world we don't understand. When we rely upon a quality of God that is unchanging, we remove the instability of self-improvement that causes exhaustion and insecurity.

For the Skeptics

Maybe leaning into God's omniscience sounds too good to be true because you have heard it all and you're a skeptic. I write this book as one myself, if that matters at all. I am far more frightened by people who never ask questions than by people who ask

God is doing the job we are attempting to do. His breath has given us life. But His life, itself, is what makes it possible for us to keep living.

God is doing the j

attempting to do.

has given us life.

life, itself, is what

too many, and I almost always play devil's advocate, even with myself.

So in case you wonder if we have to wear rose-colored glasses to believe that God knowing everything is a *good* thing, quite the opposite is true. There is value in skepticism. Skeptics question. They dig. They consider every solution before allowing themselves to be convinced. That is the place from which I've written this book. Questions (and even critiques) are often the way zealous converts to faith in Jesus first start and become most convinced about Him.

There's a lot I don't profess to know, but certain things I am increasingly sure of: God knows things we never will. He is actively working on our behalf, even when we do not realize it. Our way of trying to bring ourselves comfort and relief hasn't worked, isn't working, and won't work in the future. And God being God and us being us means that when I say, "God knows," I mean God is doing the job we are attempting to do. His breath has given us life. But His life, itself, is what makes it possible for us to keep living. *Rûaḥ to nepeš.* His Spirit breathing life into our souls, in the beginning and ongoing.

No matter why you picked up this book, we are all here for a bigger reason.

We need help.

We need comfort and relief.

We need God.

He is the only One for the job.

And He is on it.

May the skeptics be changed, the weary be renewed, and the hopeless find hope in what He knows that we do not.

Will you do something with me?

Think of the burden that sits heavy in your heart at this moment—the one that is too deep to tell even your closest person, or maybe it's the one you constantly think about.

I can't carry this anymore.

The world is overwhelming.

I don't know how to fix this problem.

I've stopped making plans for a future I can't see.

Now imagine yourself walking outside on a cloudless spring day with the wind rocking the trees in a perfect low and measured rhythm. Slowly, you lift your arms up over your head and stretch them to the sky, cracking open your fingers and letting that burden rise weightlessly into the air like a balloon, where the sky and clouds swallow it up. You watch it become less and less visible until it disappears into nonexistence.

Breathe. Exhale. Close your eyes and feel the heaviness leave your body.

If only burdens could go away this easily.

If only release was as simple as the rising of a balloon or the lifting of hands.

If only skies could swallow up real problems, fears, worries, and what-ifs.

If only.

But *what if* there were a way to finally get this kind of relief, even if the sky can't give it to us?

There is.

Keep reading.

God Knows You Need Relief

> I go east, but he is not there. I go west, but I cannot find him.
> I do not see him in the north, for he is hidden. I look to the
> south, but he is concealed. But he knows where I am going.
>
> Job 23:8–10 NLT

Everyone wants pain relief.

I suffered for years with migraines. On the limo ride to the hotel from my wedding reception I had a terrible one, lying on my new husband's lap like a wet noodle. (Welcome to marriage, honey!) You would think that would be enough to send me to a doctor, but it took winding up on a hospital floor from a vomit-inducing migraine some years later to get me to realize my headaches weren't normal and needed more than Tylenol.

Humanity is nothing if not our shared commitment to stubbornness. It seems ludicrous to walk around with physical pain symptoms if we have the privilege of things like modern medicine, but we do it all the time.

I'm too busy.

It's not that bad.

I'll do it tomorrow.

I can't find good care.

Our lack of relief may be for good reason. Sometimes there is no relief for our chronic pain after thorough pursuit, and that makes it even more maddening to watch those who could get relief but choose not to seek it. In this space, our desire for relief is often filled with grief, resentment, and ongoing questions for God.

Sometimes we've lived with our pain for so long it's like a comfortable old shoe—we don't even feel it hurting us anymore. *Oh, that's pain?* we ask, as we walk around every day with emotional bloody heels from life's blisters. For many of us, pain is our accepted new normal. We don't even know how to handle a good day anymore.

It looks different for each of us. But a comprehensive weariness seems to be the topic of almost every conversation lately. We all want God to know what we are going through and, if we're entirely honest, we want Him to do something about it. And it all centers on pain relief.

> **Our desire for relief is often filled with grief, resentment, and ongoing questions for God.**

omniscience: God's infinite knowledge and understanding of things past, present, and future.[1]

2

I don't want us to be in this spot, but we are. I don't want us to continue to think we can give ourselves pain relief by taking one more online masterclass. Resources that help us are never going to bring us the true help that can only come from God.

I want us to find lasting relief in the understanding that God's omniscience covers every type of pain we have. He knows what we are facing, what we will face, and even more than we could ever think to worry or wonder about—and has that covered too.

Finding Comfort

If I were to ask, "Why don't you seek help for your fear, loneliness, grief, worry, and questions?" you might reply that you have. You might show me all your receipts from trying.

Or on the other hand, you might give me these answers:

No one can fix it.

I can't trust anyone to help me.

People have let me down.

You may be right about this, since it involves other humans. Ultimately, as good as therapy can be, by itself, it can't fix your heart. As present and trustworthy as other people are capable of being, they will at some point fail to save you.

If I were to ask, "Where do you go to find relief when you are afraid, lonely, grieving, *worried, and wondering?" I suspect I would hear these answers:*

To my friends.

To church leadership.

To counseling.

To my phone/the internet.
To Netflix.
To_____ (enter substance of choice).

It's interesting, isn't it? We live rather inconsistently, even about our pain. We have failed history with people, but we still go to them for solutions. Things have never brought us permanent comfort, yet we continue to rely upon them. While the One who knows everything about our lives is often our last resort.

If you know the story of Job, you know that if there was a pain Olympics, Job would qualify for the gold. Knowing that he has had nearly everything he loved taken away from him helps me appreciate even more his words in Job 23:8–10: "I go east, but he is not there. I go west, but I cannot find him. I do not see him in the north, for he is hidden. I look to the south, but he is concealed. But he knows where I am going" (NLT).

Job is dealing with true heartache, having lost his health, his possessions, and his entire family. He wants to go and find God to talk to Him personally (v. 3). He is honest, and I appreciate that. I need someone who can relate to my pain so I know that he is human and that he feels what I feel: "My complaint today is still a bitter one, and I try hard not to groan aloud," he says, candidly (v. 2 NLT). He is saying things we all have felt.

I've read the book of Job hundreds of times in my life, but these verses fall fresh on me this time. How can a man who has gone through so much, who is feeling as if God is MIA— nowhere to be found—find comfort and relief from such a Source? Job tells us in these seven words: "But he knows where I am going" (Job 23:10).

But *He knows*. These are words of assurance even in questioning. Confidence during crisis. Job finds comfort in the understanding that even though he couldn't see Him, feel Him, or find Him, God knew his current location and future path. He trusted in God with unseen confidence. And it gave him pain relief.

You might not be able to see it right now. Does God feel hidden? Perhaps you have a bitter complaint and you are trying hard not to groan aloud, or maybe you *are* groaning. That's okay. God fully accepts groans. There may be a few things you'd love to say to God, or maybe you already have (again okay, because He can handle it). You don't have to understand *how* God knows where you are going or what you are going through. You just have to believe that *He does*.

Belief is important; then the practice of that belief plays out in release. Release is a crucial part of pain relief. That is why the thought of releasing our worries into the air like balloons, if that could bring us true relief, sounds incredible—it's an easy way to do what is a much harder practice for our soul. The irony is most of us want pain relief, but we grab tightly to the things that could relieve us from it. It's natural instinct, even though it's counterintuitive. Babies grind their teeth when they are teething, even though biting farther into tender gums makes the gums hurt worse. Holding on when you need to let go doesn't work for parenthood, waterskiing, or managing your own life. But it's what we do.

> But *He knows*. These are words of assurance even in questioning. Confidence during crisis.

When we struggle to release things, it's not always because we simply don't trust other people's abilities or that we trust ourselves too much. It could be because we've attempted release in the context of the temporary. Some of us have tried to change something by sheer will or simple wish, and those things come with good intention and occasional fanfare—but they don't last long. True release is only possible with an accompanying depth of belief in something lasting. We can only forgo what burdens us to Someone omniscient enough to handle it. And that's not us.

Night Terrors and Nahum

Five years ago, two noteworthy things happened to me.

The first thing was night terrors. Despite prayer and counseling, I still sometimes experience them. They come as bad dreams, or sometimes I am simply jolted awake by fear. Often, as I pray through them, God speaks to me both during and after them. I am only able to go back to sleep with His assurance that He has me and my family, and we are okay.

I have come to believe night terrors are a part of how Satan attacks me in the night as I work on projects for the kingdom of God. If he can frighten me enough to stop me, he takes one more person out of the game. His goal is always to destroy us, and mental anguish is a primary method.

Around the same time the night terrors started, another event of spiritual significance took place. Similar to the night terrors, this appeared to come out of the blue. This time, though, it was a gift from God. He spoke to me about something very specifically while I was in church.

I heard Him say these words to my heart: *I want you to study the book of Nahum.* The pastor wasn't preaching on Nahum, nor had I seen it recently referenced somewhere, so I could determine no subconscious prompting. Sometimes people ask me, "How can I know I am hearing from God?" Often my experience has been very simply like this: He says things I would not say to myself. I wouldn't have told myself to study Nahum. If you've ever read the book, you know why.

Nahum is a short, three-chapter Old Testament collection of prophetic poems, sandwiched between Habakkuk and Micah, the seventh book of the twelve Minor Prophets. It has a lot of strong words in it like *burning fury, destruction,* and *crushed*—not a book I am typically drawn to in my Bible reading and certainly not during wearying times of life. At the time, when I was experiencing night terrors, this book felt particularly harsh and uncomfortable. I needed to read Psalms, not Nahum. I needed God to love and comfort me, not remind me I needed to repent. This was a confusing biblical narrative. "Why would you send me here, God?" I often asked out loud while reading the book.

But while we judge things by the surface, God knows the subplot.

The words of Nahum look harsh, but the deeper picture of Nahum is a representation of life: things don't always look like they really are. God knows what we don't. And God is taking care of it. Even reading it was a reminder to me that I don't know what I think I do.

> But while we judge things by the surface, God knows the subplot.

Nahum: a name derived from the verb מחנ (nchm), meaning "comfort."[2]

7

I wanted comfort for my night terrors. It appeared Nahum would be the last place to look. Was God oblivious to my needs? *Not at all*. Nahum's name, itself, means comfort and relief, and God knew exactly what He was doing when He had me read it. I could only believe that the timing of my night terrors and reading Nahum was a coincidence if I didn't believe God knows.

Isn't this so often our testimony: God knew when we did not? What we assumed He was doing wasn't what He was actually doing?

On the surface, Nahum is a message from God to the people in the Assyrian capital city of Nineveh. They were in grave trouble for their horrific abuses of the people of Judah, which He had not missed. But the story beneath that story? God's assurance of rescue. God's plan is always thorough like that. Nothing is hidden from Him, and there is nothing that will not be made right.

Only seven verses into the first chapter of Nahum, it's all there. Very plainly, while all the things are burning and blazing and crumbling and quaking, there is this short word that's everything: "The LORD is good, a stronghold in the day of trouble; And He knows those who trust in Him" (NKJV).

The Lord is good.

God knows.

Maybe your pain is coming from a place in your past, and you need to believe God will make right what you cannot.

Maybe it's coming from your need to believe in something again after you've had hope after hope and dream after dream crushed.

Maybe you are gripped by fear or consumed by the pain of loss and you're holding on so tightly because you believe holding on helps you control the things that feel out of your control.

God's message to you is that He knows where you are going, even when you can't see or feel or find Him, just like Job.

God's message to you is that He knows where you are going, even when you can't see or feel or find Him, just like Job.

He is asking you to trust Him for the relief you may not be able to see, but it will come, just like it did for the people of Judah.

If you don't know where to start with this, read to the end of the chapter and I'll give you some practical ways to begin.

What You Know to Be True About Life Versus What You Know to Be True About God

In many ways, I am not the same person I was five years ago. I'm confident you're not the same person you were five years ago either, at the very least, because of the unpredictability of life. Most of us couldn't have seen a lot of our lives coming. We imagine, we dream, we hope. But we aren't future-tellers by planning and projection alone (or in any way).

Belief can be based on hope, desires, and even life trajectories and symptoms. ("I believe I will live in the city and have a great corporate job in finance.") *Experience* is based on our reality. ("I live in the suburbs and run an online business from home.") Often, what we once believed looks very different from what we actually live now.

It's not a flaw to be wrong about how our life has turned out.

There is a problem, however, when we think life is all about us—when we either take the credit for our lives or we allow ourselves constant excuses for them. Choice, certainly, is ours to own, and so is living in some type of faulty belief system. But there's a difference between that and the realities of life in a flawed world in which sometimes things happen to us without our permission.

The reason we are often wrong about where we will be in five years is that while we make daily choices to lead us on a path, we cannot know other factors out of our control that will come into play that inform even the best-laid plans and decisions. It's also why the illusion of control is more damaging than we may realize: it creates within us the pressure to make perfect decisions with the belief that whatever is wrong, we can make right by our own hands. Then when we don't, we endlessly blame ourselves because we should have been more capable.

> Often, what we once believed looks very different from what we actually live now.

God knowing (and you not) should be of comfort to you. You might have been blaming yourself for a long time for things only God could have ever seen coming, and this is the moment to finally find relief from that mental shift.

It's amazing what perspective can bring, even in the form of a small reminder. When we carry around the weight that we have failed because our life isn't what we predicted, remembering that we aren't in control of the world can remove unnecessary burdens. We might have made some different choices had we known then what we know now. Or maybe not. But we were never meant to hold any of this together. We never could. We took on a job we were destined to fail. It's simply too big, which is why God never asked us to bear it.

Of course, not all our problems are due to things we couldn't have seen coming. We may need to admit to God that we knew good and well and still went headfirst into a bad

> You might have been blaming yourself for a long time for things only God could have ever seen coming, and this is the moment to finally find relief from that mental shift.

choice, or we were trying to do His job. Run after that pain relief in the form of repentance and confession. It's the best relief in the world, and trust me, I know it well.

Speaking of the difference between *belief* and *experience*, what we *believe* about God is different from what we know to be true about Him, which is about our *experience* with Him. Head versus heart. We can believe God is love because we have read that somewhere in the Bible or trust what our parents have taught us about Him. But what we ultimately know to be true about God's love is what we've personally experienced. Familiarity. We know the landmarks—the sights, smells, and sounds. Been there, lived that. How He has loved us in the dark, in our hard-to-love times. To truly feel the things we crave—steadied, loved, strong, comforted—we have to have firsthand experience with them. They can't be far-off cognitive concepts. They have to be things we've felt deep inside our bones when we couldn't provide them for ourselves—the mystery of God's hand on us in ways we cannot explain in words. Otherwise, it's just a nice thought. Nice thoughts don't help us in our hardships.

Here's where it can get dicey but is absolutely crucial.

Presenting issue

VS.

What you know to be true
about life (past that has
informed you)

What you know to be true
about God (places he has
been true to you)

copyright Lisa Whittle

In the world in which we live, especially during difficult times, there will always be a competition inside us between what we know to be true about God and what we know to be true about life. In the hardest of times, these ideas will be in fierce competition. They will compete for our peace. They will compete for our minds. They will compete for our endurance and joy. We'll not only need to have a point of reference to draw upon with God that can rival what we know about life, it will need to be *the more profound experience*. When we spend life pouring into experiences that merely mimic the fullness of Christ, we can begin to believe in, and even crave, a faux profound experience of a life outside of Him. It will become the life that most informs our thinking when hardships come, which leads to shaky ground.

What we believe about God is different from what we know to be true about Him.

It is also why in our faith communities—the church—we must not settle for lazy discipleship.

Because a shallow faith built on hype will never experience God as the true *more profound experience* in life—thus, faith in Him will always be an accoutrement rather than the foundation. This type of faith isn't enough to weather hard times, let alone produce faithfulness.

On the other hand, when we experience *Jesus as our most profound experience* in life, everything changes, and it makes all the difference for pain relief. It does not remove all aspects of complication; as John 16:33 promises, "In this world you will have trouble." But it underlines the second part of that verse, making it most important: "But take heart! I have overcome the world." Do not hear what I'm saying to mean that Jesus is in any way in competition with anything to be more profound—there is no true competition. He *is* the most profound. But He will not force us to know that. It's only when we have experienced Him that we find true pain relief rather than settle for a theoretical comfort that God knows what is happening in our lives. And for Him to show us these important benefits to our life (Him = The Benefit from which all benefits such as peace, joy, and hope flow), we have to be open to Him. Allow Him access. Give Him opportunity. So if we can't vouch for God's sufficiency in our life, a good starting point is to take a look at the access we've given Him to be sufficient.

When you know God in the highs, you begin to see His face in the lows. The reverse is also true; in a deepened walk with Christ, highs and lows become less about our emotions and more about us experiencing *Him*. This too creates trust. Give Him the chance and He will not fail to be compelling. Again, in the context of pain relief, as we are compelled by God, release becomes easier. But do not expect His being compelling to meet

It's only when we have experienced Him that we find true pain relief rather than settle for a theoretical comfort that God knows what is happening in our lives.

your stereotype. Those mountaintop moments are wonderful, but so are the moments when we are desperate in a ditch and His is the only face we can see. Firsthand experience with God will always make for stronger believers, not weaker ones, so there is no risk here.

You are not wrong to want pain relief—you are human. I hope you'll begin to see how God's omniscience is both tender and powerful for you—both timeless and current, global and personal. It is an invitation for God to prove true in your life and also be believed for who He is. It is a comfort for where you are but also a nudge to move you to a place of greater strength and understanding.

God will always weep with you. But He also wants more victory for you in the present, more joy, less sorrow. He has watched you go to bed far too many nights and wept with you over all the things that He knows only one of you can handle. You will not get relief without removing the other comforts and letting Him be enough.

> Those mountaintop moments are wonderful, but so are the moments when we are desperate in a ditch and His is the only face we can see.

Real Life

Darling Holly. I can still see the brown-eyed, curly-haired young woman who wore the perma-smile the whole time she spoke of her pain, which instinct told me was most certainly her MO. I imagined she was the *I'm fine, don't worry about me* one, a lot.

She was far younger than I, but I wanted to be her friend and her mama all at the same time. I tried to send her this message with my eyes from across the room.

When I met Holly, I was going through a season in my ministry in which, when gathering with women, I often asked them this question: "What is the greatest need of your heart right now?" Frankly, I never quite knew what I was going to hear. You might think women would phone it in rather than speak their hearts, but they rarely did that. Almost always, honesty rolled out with their tears, maybe because pain is pushier these days or maybe because we have gotten over trying to lie to people about it.

There were about ten of us sitting around, including Holly. Holly was in the middle of the pack, but with every woman's answer, I saw her eyes getting more and more glassy, looking like a cup with water at its brim, about to overflow. We finally got to her as our eyes locked. Suddenly the smile stopped, her head lowered, and she breathed out words that were quiet but unmistakable, "I feel forgotten." The air stood still in the room. One small fly buzzed around, but no one had the strength to kill it. A barely detectable groan broke the silence. A chorus of silent nods. Holly had outed our worst-kept secret: we've all felt forgotten.

In a quick flash of regret, I felt suddenly foolish, having led this young woman to share such a vulnerability. How dare I intrude on our secret. None of us was ready for this after just meeting over pork nachos. Or maybe . . . *I* wasn't.

I thought back to my own experience of feeling forgotten by my mother when I was in middle school—a silly nothing in the scheme of life. Uber attentive, she was horrified about this mistake. She only forgot to pick me up at school once that I can remember, but I still remember it. She eventually barreled in, frazzled and apologetic, an hour later, and all was forgiven with two crunchy tacos from Taco Bell. It was so minor. But anytime you feel the insecurity of being forgotten, it makes its mark.

Many of us are carrying around this pain. So the idea that God knows—about our grief, our dreams, our past, those hardships and injustices—is appealing but not altogether comforting. Not when we feel like *He* is the One who has forgotten us. This is where most of our internal wrestling stems from. He doesn't appear to be hearing our requests or even our painful pleadings. *Help me, God.* Crickets. *Show me, God.* Silence. *Make it right, God.* Not so much as a flicker of change can we see.

This is real, but it is also not fatal. We are not relegated to a life where we have to choose between being happy about God's silence in our lives *or* being resentful of it. His knowledge of our circumstances is a fact that doesn't change, but His heart can be moved by prayer. (We will talk more about Hezekiah later in the book, where we'll see a great example of this in 2 Kings 20:5, when God says: "I have heard your prayer and seen your tears; I will heal you.")

This also does not mean God will automatically, or even always, do what we want. His ways, thoughts, and knowledge are on a different plane than ours, so our requests will be made with limited knowledge, and it's foolish to assume our best wisdom could match His unlimited knowledge with that. ("'My thoughts are not your thoughts, neither are your ways my ways,' declares the LORD" [Isaiah 55:8].) So many dreams I thought I wanted. So many moments I begged Him to say yes to my prayers. Most of those things I am grateful I never got.

And always, our response to His actions (even His silence, which is an action), shapes and changes us. So as we experience the emotion of feeling forgotten, our response to that emotion develops a deeper faith—or it can draw us further away from it.

> We are not relegated to a life where we have to choose between being happy about God's silence in our lives *or* being resentful of it.

Emotions are also real, and God is tender to them. *Of course* we would be much better at our spiritual relationship if our sight were able to confirm God's activity in our lives. It just rarely does, because "Faith is the confidence that what we hope for will actually happen; it gives us assurance about things we cannot see" (Hebrews 11:1 NLT). And I have to believe this, as with all things God designed, was on purpose and for our good, even though we cannot comprehend it. Trust and belief in that does not require me to understand the *why*. I find Hebrews 11:1 to be among God's greatest heads-ups that His inner workings on macro (corporate, world) and micro (personal, individual) levels will often not be provable. At least, not for some period of time. The truth is simply this: we find it hard to release things to God because we struggle with two very present realities: the way we *feel* and the way things *seem*, both of which are aspects directly tied to what we know to be true about life. Remember, when what we know to be true about life becomes the more profound experience than what we know to be true about God, we struggle.

Holly spoke to the feelings—what she knew to be true about her own life. She shared feelings we all have, doubting God because we *feel* forgotten by Him. *Our* feelings. This is when a deep belief in His omniscience—an unchanging attribute—being active and at work in a full picture of our lives comes into play. We know we remain on His mind, and so do our circumstances, even when we feel otherwise.

We are always going to have problems when we feel like we don't have a future. Our feelings may very convincingly say that God has abandoned us. We might even start believing that He doesn't know what's best for us, or know our situation, or care about us at all.

It's not that those feelings aren't real. But if you trust them more than you trust God's plans for you, you withhold your own relief from pain.

Pain Release

It's quiet. You're not sitting in a circle in a room with ten women. No one is putting you on the spot. It's just you and God. So let me ask you:

What is the greatest need of your heart right now?

I still find this an important question. It's crucial to acknowledge it and discuss it with God. He knows anyway. But bringing it into the open with Him can help you deal with it yourself.

After you've considered this a bit, a next question:

What do you know to be true about God?

And then, a last one:

Right now, which is your more profound experience—what you know to be true about life or what you know to be true about God?

Your life, how you are dealing with your pain, how much

you trust that God knows, is probably telling you the answers to these questions already.

"The more you know the more peace you will have" is a lie.

Knowledge doesn't automatically bring peace. Sometimes knowledge brings anxiety, distrust, and fear. Certainly in this information age, knowledge hasn't made us happier and more peaceful. Quite the opposite.

"The more you know the more you can control" is a lie.

If this were true, we would be able to control every disease known to humankind just by googling it. We could make our kids be completely safe or make the right decision just by knowing their location. *If only.*

And on the other hand of this control issue? The call to know nothing. Simply bury our head in the sand and deflect from our problems. Numb out. Pretend the pain doesn't matter. Be mad at everyone. Act out in another way. Make our real issues about something else.

There is a third option: to live with the relief that God knows instead of us.

I realize that might feel scary at first. Maybe you've been holding on and doing it your way for a long time. But looking to God for relief is not ignorance; it's wisdom. Resistance blocks release. Release leads to relief. Relief brings peace. Write that down somewhere. Think about it. Pray about it.

I understand wanting to know why things happen. I get that it seems like if we could only understand the reason or change something, we would be a happier, more fulfilled, more peaceful people. I relate to feeling like pain relief will need to be on my terms.

But please consider the heart of Solomon, the wisest man

who ever lived. He gave firsthand
testimony of this truth: God's
intimate knowledge of our lives,
combined with His deep and abiding
love for us, means that sometimes
He chooses to keep things from us.

> But looking to God for relief is not ignorance; it's wisdom.

And while we might *think* knowing those things would bring us
peace, often the opposite is true. Trusting that God knows the
things that we don't is the safest place we can be.

I said to myself, "Look, I have increased in wisdom more
than anyone who has ruled over Jerusalem before me; I have
experienced much of wisdom and knowledge." Then I applied
myself to the understanding of wisdom, and also of madness
and folly, but I learned that this, too, is a chasing after the
wind. For with much wisdom comes much sorrow; the more
knowledge, the more grief. (Ecclesiastes 1:16–18)

Only God can bring us the pain relief we need because only
He knows how much we need, when we need it, and in what
form we need it to be.

Because God knows my pain, I can turn to Him for relief.

Relief: 3 Steps to Move Forward

1. Start a list of the areas in which you need pain relief. Next to each item, write down how God's omniscience in Scripture helps you with that particular pain point.
2. Make two columns—what you know to be true about life and what you know to be true about God. Then write down which is your most profound experience and why.
3. Write a short prayer expressing your desire to believe that God knows about your situation, asking Him to help you look to Him for your relief—it can even be five to ten words. Every day for thirty days, pray this prayer of intention. He hears you and will honor your pure heart's desire.

God Knows Your Dreams

We make our own plans, but the LORD
decides where we will go.
Proverbs 16:9 CEV

I remember very clearly when my father, a dreamer by nature, stopped dreaming. No longer a pastor, he was living in isolation out on a remote gravel road in a season of forced sabbatical after losing his church. Because he had a court case with the IRS splashed across the news, no one would want to touch him again with a ten-foot pole. His ministry life was surely over. He no longer talked in terms of things he wanted to do, see, or hoped to grow old and stick around for. Instead, he started to speak in facts. The gleam of the thin place where childhood imagination meets adult ambition left his eye. Hearing him no longer live in the context of his dreams made me feel, in my own way, less hopeful. When you lose the wonder of possibility, you not only lose your own joy, but also the ability to inspire others.

For months dad was a man without dreams. And then one day he said to me out of the blue, "Lisa, I have an idea about something," and I knew his hopes were returning. His ideas had always been sparked by a belief in possibility, and they had come back. There was a new dream in there, but it was more tentative, a little wiser. He was not the same dreamer. That *him* had been broken, or maybe, made better by allowing his once random dreams to mold into more reasonable hopes. Either way, his spirit was awakened. The gleam in his eye was once again present. Possibility had revisited him.

> When you lose the wonder of possibility, you not only lose your own joy, but also the ability to inspire others.

Dreaming about our life is a sign we are still in it.

I don't know whether you consider yourself in or out of your life at this point, but I want you to be in. I want you to know that dreams are not just for some of us, but for everyone who still has breath in his or her lungs. The *rûaḥ* of God makes that possible.

God's omniscience plays a huge role in our dreaming. As He knows the things we are hoping for, He is exercising His attribute of unlimited insight and wisdom to bridle, guide, and funnel those dreams in the best, right direction. This is a beautiful picture of our free will and desires meeting the surrender of prayer for His guidance. Sometimes we will sense His guiding hand; sometimes we will not even know how or where He is guiding us, even as we are led. When we trust that God knowing includes unforeseen leadership that is for our good out of His love for us, we can better accept that when a dream doesn't work out, there is something He knew that we did not. Of course, this is much easier on paper. But the history of this practice proves its worthiness.

Dreaming about our life is a sign we are still in it.

More than one time in my life, I have been grateful for the reality of Proverbs 16:9: "We make our own plans, but the LORD decides where we will go" (CEV). Had God allowed many of the plans I had dreamed up to come to fruition, I would be living a very different reality today.

We all need dreams to engage in our life.

We all need God to guide those dreams instead of us.

We all need to trust that He knows better about them than we do.

We All Dream Differently

We are quite a melting pot of people with different feelings about dreams.

Some of us are *realists*, or at least that is what we like to call ourselves. We believe in dreams but can consider ourselves too busy or too practical for them. Working hard is our sweet spot. Even visionaries like me who live in thoughts five to ten years down the road often struggle to have dreams for ourselves. Sometimes we see dreams as conflicts to tangible efforts, and dreamers as wild-eyed and uncommitted. Sometimes disappointment has turned us into those realists without space to dream. But hope is not just for those with laid-back personalities and lighter schedules. Realists can (and should) dream too.

And there are the *dreamers by nature*—those who have no problem dreaming of their lives. The issue for a dreamer is a little different; it is at times hard to channel those aspirations well, condense them to valuable efforts, and discern which are best uses of gifts and talents. As a dreamer, you believe in yourself and your dreams, and I love that about you. You are in many ways at your best when dreaming up creative, wonderful things. But in that space, sometimes you view those who have a more linear way of doing things with a critical eye, and when they don't share your enthusiasm for new dreams, you may even shy away from them.

And then there are the *former dreamers*—those of you who used to dream but have stopped. We could fill the chapter with what rug might have been pulled out from under you to stop you from dreaming. Maybe you've been jaded by someone or something and you feel like it's no longer worth the risk of having any more dreams. My friend, *it is*. You don't have to choose between self-protection and the hope of possibility. You don't need to stop dreaming in order to put food on the table. It's a both/and. Needs are real, *and* dreaming is self-care.

So you can see, this issue of dreams has us resting in somewhat different places. We are in need of God's knowledge about how dreams play out in our individual lives; we need Him to be the Anchor we trust more than even our own opinions about our dreams.

God places high value on dreams.

Never doubt that God esteems dreams. Multiple times in the Bible (twenty-one recorded dreams) He used a dream to do game-changing things like send a crucial message or spare a life.

Joseph, the favorite son of Jacob, was no *average* dreamer in Genesis. In addition to the normal dreams he surely had for his own life, Joseph experienced prophetic dreams that would require God's omniscience to come to fulfillment. They were simply too lofty and far-fetched, otherwise. Joseph's dreams—that his family would bow to him in a future position of authority—must have seemed like those of a boy living in a fantasy world of his own ego, especially when he was just seventeen years old at the time. His brothers already resented him for being the most beloved, given the colorful coat by his father as a gesture of his overt favoritism. I'm sure they were skeptical at best that Joseph's dream was anything more than just a silly projection of subliminal wishes—at worst, to flaunt his privilege among them.

Oh yes, there was pushback. Sometimes when we have dreams that God puts inside our hearts, though they may not be as clearly prophetic as Joseph's, we will share them with someone and we will feel unsupported or even resisted in that dream we believe to be from God. It will hurt, and we often question ourselves in light of the pushback. But we must trust that God is leading us. And in that personal relationship, outside opinion isn't necessary.

The dream to rule over Joseph's brothers wasn't his dream. It was God's vision for him. But it still got Joseph in trouble. His brothers sold him into slavery. He wrongly ended up in prison. There, he also interpreted dreams; God was the source of both the dreams and the gift to discern them. Joseph quickly rose to become trusted and favored by Pharaoh (ruler in Egypt) for this gift, and Pharaoh put Joseph in charge of all Egypt. In the end, the dream God gave Joseph when he was seventeen did in fact come true, with his brothers bowing down to him as their ruler. A most incredible full circle.

So what can we learn from Joseph's dreams?

1. Dreams from God cannot be carried out without Him.
2. We must be walking closely with God to discern when dreams are from Him and to walk with confidence when dreams He gives us aren't met with outside approval.
3. God's dreams for us will often begin to feel like dreams for ourselves as we desire the same things He desires for our lives, in our reliance on Him.

You aren't alone with your dreams. God was in them before you.

sovereignty: God is free and able to do what He wants; His all-encompassing rule over the entire universe.[1]

God wants us to trust Him throughout our dreaming.

As with many things in life, we often start out great in the beginning, but we taper off after a while. A lot of us love to involve God in our dreams when we are praying for fresh vision or a new plan, but we are less willing to keep consulting Him once we have gotten things underway. Our solo instinct rears its head and we run off, but His sovereignty is thorough. He knows not only the germination of a dream but also how it needs to be watered and given oxygen to grow and flourish. He even knows how it needs to end well, if it comes to that.

I have watched God, personally, take my husband and me through that process with starting and closing a church. To this

You aren't alone
with your dreams.
God was in them
before you.

You aren't alo

with your drea

God was in the

before you

day, I can't tell you for sure if the dream to start it came from Him or us. But I am confident that He knew about how to help us end it well. It was one of the things that concerned me greatly, and God helping us see that dream come to a close was the only way we didn't make a complete mess of it.

This too is important to note, because with the responsibility of dreams comes the wisdom to defer them to the ultimate Dream-Giver. Even our minds that have the capacity to dream belong to God. We can run ahead of God with things we dream up, but if we don't rely on God to manage them, those things will never have the same impact.

Sometimes we may wonder if a dream is from God or from us. That is completely normal. It is also why staying in a close, intimate relationship with Jesus is crucial; as the Holy Spirit leads us, we have a sense of what things are from Him and not us.

What dreams have you trusted God with all the way through?

Even our minds that have the capacity to dream belong to God.

What dreams have you tried to manage, at any point in the process, even when He could handle them better?

Through the years I've had a lot of dreams I have tried to make work, to my own detriment. I've dreamed about boys I never married, successes I never achieved, homes I never lived in, words I never heard, and places I've never been. Sometimes those dreams kept me going until God gave me a new dream. Other times the dream died, and I was sad. But I have never regretted trusting God with my dreams. And I have never regretted a life where I got the privilege of dreaming, because that meant my life felt *possible*.

It is a lie to believe that our dreams have to work out every time exactly like we want them to in order to be worthy to have been dreamed. We get to dream. Maybe that is enough for today.

It is a lie to believe that our dreams have to work out every time exactly like we want them to in order to be worthy to have been dreamed.

dream: a cherished aspiration, ambition, or ideal.[2]

God dream: a calling involving purpose that is prompted outside of personal ambition.

prophetic dream: term usually used to reference dreams of foresight from God about future events or dreams that contain supernatural messages.[3]

When You Leave God Out of Your Dream

There's a flash of a scene that plays insignificantly in the beginning credits of the iconic nineties movie *Pretty Woman*. A man's voice yelling into the air at no one in particular, "Welcome to Hollywood. What's your dream?"

Isn't that how we often see dreams? Yelling into the air of hopefulness? Bright lights, big-city flashiness? In stark reality, my dreams have been far more unseen, sacred, and quiet than that. It might take tenacity to see dreams through, but dreams themselves are usually quite fragile. We care about them. They are a part of us—a part of whom we hope to become.

Most of our dreams are about some piece of our identity, which is why we feel so closely tied to them—and often so insecure. Our dreams can begin to take on personalities of their own—boss us around and dictate how we live our lives, what road we take next, even how we see ourselves when they don't work out like we envision them. This is why we have to anchor them to Christ. It is why trusting His omniscience about our dreams is critical. We see dreams with our eyes and desires. He sees dreams in the realm of His sovereignty.

We can love a dream so much that it becomes a god. Anything can. Good dreams can. Important dreams. Right dreams. Beautiful dreams. God has to stay at the center of our dreams so that doesn't happen.

Because remember, dreams in Scripture are kingdom-focused—about God's intention and vision for the ideal of humanity rather than individual pursuits. This tells us that though God ordained dreams, they were not for greater personal indulgence. As humans, we are adept at coming up with ways to turn even the best gifts from God for His purposes into gifts solely to serve ourselves. Even as, in His love for us, He longs to give us "the desires of [our] heart" (Psalm 37:4), which would often include our dreams. It is in the context of that desire coming under the *first* priority of daily obedience to Christ. This kind of right life-ordering drives right life-dreaming. As we obey Him, the pursuit of the kingdom of God becomes our primary heart's desire—and that will shape the rest of our dreams.

To put it simply, God doesn't want to be tacked onto the end of our dreams. We've all seen people pursue dreams "in the name of Jesus," and maybe we've done that sometimes too. But there should be a greater reverence to dreams than that. There should be a deeper understanding of the interworking of desire, calling, ideas, and God's omniscience of it all. He's the only One who could weave the entire process together. And though He created us individually and sees and loves us as such, His coming to earth and death and resurrection was a corporate plan for creation. Individualization of the plan—the "dream" of God, then—disorients us from our created self. Orienting our dreams into the larger "dream" of Jesus is what allows us to be free to live personal dreams for ourselves. Otherwise, we are like the Hollywood guy yelling out into the air to no one in particular, *"What's your dream?"* all floating around with no rhyme or reason to the whims we pursue.

Without God, dreams can become unanchored wishes. With God, dreams are purposeful wants.

God wants nothing more than for our desires to morph with His—our dreams to be in sync. Desire is biblical. When He is our top desire, our dreams are not at risk of going rogue into self-satisfying ventures. This is of great benefit because it gives us the freedom to dream without the concern we are excluding God from it. And it also changes the way we approach dreaming. We find much more wisdom and structure to support the idea and passion.

Without God, dreams can become unanchored wishes. With God, dreams are purposeful wants.

immutability: His freedom from change and His being the same at all times past, present, and future.[4]

Allowing God to ground our dreams in His immutability takes us from frenzied to focused. In other words, we would be fools to leave God out. It makes no sense to exclude the management of our life from the hopes we have for it. There is no true separation of the two.

If you haven't had a dream work out like you wanted, join the club. I've had too many to count. I have often discovered that a particular dream was a mental distraction. I craved the rush of a dream when I was bored in my relationship with God or dissatisfied with life. What I really needed was to stop thinking about what could be and focus on how I needed God to change me. Dead-end dreams can draw us to Christ.

Jesus followers can still live for ourselves, but we will never ultimately have peace about it. A measure of satisfaction in the fruition of a dream isn't automatically a sign of God's approval. We can gain some pleasure and joy in things that have little to do with Him. Don't assume because a dream came true it was a gift from God.

All of this undoubtedly bears the question: Is there a foolproof way to know if the dream is God's or ours? If it is okay with Him or not?

Here's where it gets very simple. You know your life purpose from Matthew 28:19, which is to go and make disciples. You know the circumstances of your life by which you are living out that purpose. And you know if the dream you have is moving you closer to that or further away.

God Isn't a Doorman to Our Dreams

This is a good place to pause and address an area of accepted, yet widely misunderstood theology that affects how we dream: the idea that God is simply a doorman to them.

The thought that God will open and close doors when it comes to our dreams and thinking that open doors merely represent God's approval and closed doors merely represent God's restriction is something many of us subscribe to. Christians have an obsession with this door analogy. But the truth is actually much bigger (and far better) than what we think.

Doors are deeply significant in Scripture. They are mentioned roughly four hundred times throughout the Old and New Testaments in both literal and figurative ways.[5] But it's not just about doors as opportunities or non-opportunities— relegated to a mode of communication from God. The concept of the door was, in Scripture, those things as well. But it also represented much more—freedom, faith, and judgment, to name a few.

Get ready, because here's where it really gets good.

In the most incredible mention of a door in Scripture, Christ calls *Himself* a door in John 10:9: "I am the door. If anyone enters by me, he will be saved and will go in and out and find pasture" (ESV). In context, He had been previously illustrating in John 10:1–2 the other ways people try to get to heaven in a metaphor of tending to the sheep: "Truly, truly, I say to you, he who does not enter the sheepfold by the door but climbs in by another way, that man is a thief and a robber. But he who enters by the door is the shepherd of the sheep" (ESV).

My goodness, if we haven't tried to enter through some other "doors."

God is not only *not* a mere doorman to help you get to heaven, but He is *not* a doorman to your dreams in the interim—some spiritual valet, opening and closing doors for you, accommodating hopes, plans, ideas, and wishes.

He *is* the door. He *is* the dream.

35

The kingdom of God is the dream—it is not a means to your individual dream, as we've already covered.

Since this is true and this is His role, it is also true that we will be the most fulfilled in our lives when we are living in the context of the Dream, Jesus, and when we are living our dreams in the context of the kingdom-dream He has for us.

God might be using a closed or open door in your life to communicate with you about something, but do not see doors as merely that. See them as places to exercise your faith. Where you are giving priority and authority. Where you are seeing Jesus love, protect, care for, and relentlessly pursue you. Where He is offering you freedom. And yes, where He is opening up opportunities in your life.[6] There is action on your part in a door. Your effort on the other side of God's sovereignty is crucial.

> God is not your doorman. He is the Door to everything you have ever wanted and more.

God is not your doorman. He is the Door to everything you have ever wanted and more.

> **goal**: the object of a person's ambition or effort; an aim or desired result.[7]

Dreams Versus Goals

Knowing the difference between a dream and a goal is important.

A lot of us are walking around feeling like our dreams never come true—when we have mistaken a dream for a goal we no longer have the heart for. If it's the latter, it's in your best interest that the thing you thought was an unfulfilled dream never worked out. It starts with asking yourself this question: *Is that really what my heart longs for, or a goal I once had I can't let go?*

My goal was once to be a psychologist. But one day I realized it wasn't really my dream, even though I had been calling it that. My heart didn't long for it anymore. At twenty-three, I felt the call of God on my life to preach. I didn't want to, because it didn't seem practical or possible. I had my "dreams" of becoming a psychologist, my goals with my schooling, and my ideas about what women could and couldn't be used to do for God. Preaching didn't fit into that.

The interesting thing is how much the call of God on my life would utilize some of the prior schooling, equipping, and tools I had for what my heart really longed for. I didn't know at the time I would go on to write books, travel, and preach. But sometimes dreams and goals intersect in ways we didn't foresee, but ways intimately known by God. If I truly believe God wastes nothing, I know that even the things I did in preparation for a goal I never met became useful. Situations like these are where "God knows" moves from a lofty concept to a real-life testimonial.

Know the difference.

Your dreams and goals may be two different things. Maybe you've been thinking one was really the other. Or maybe your dreams and goals look similar, or even merge or cross over. Sometimes they are hard to tell apart.

I know a young woman who had her heart set on one day marrying a specific young man. For years it had been more than a bucket-list hope—she'd always said it was her dream. She'd written his name on pieces of paper with hers, imagined their kids, and pinned their perfect wedding on Pinterest. Even when she was dating other guys, in her mind, he was the one. After graduating from college, she started working in a big city and eventually met someone new. He enhanced her life, challenged her in the best ways, and she eventually fell in love with him. But she struggled because her dream of marrying the boy from the past lived long in her mind. She came to me to ask me what to do when she found herself having conversations with this new guy about marriage. "It's been my dream for so long to marry my dream guy. How can I give that up, even though I love my boyfriend?" I saw the dilemma in her eyes. I understood her concern. It's hard to let go of something you've held in your heart for so long.

Eventually she came to see that even if it was a dream of hers at one point, at another point it had become a goal she couldn't let go of. It was driving her, keeping her focused on achieving it. She wanted to get what always seemed to elude her. But it was also hindering her from the love that was true and real. My young friend married the new man, and her dream to be loved happened after all—just not with the boy from the past.

Don't let your goals get in the way of where God is leading you now. It's not a failure to never reach a goal. It's unwise to keep reaching for it when it is no longer the best thing for you.

I relate to my friend, but with houses. My dream was always to design and build my own home. It kept not working out for us to do it, and I finally had to ask myself, *Why do I keep pushing for this?* I knew that even if it started out as a dream, it wasn't really what my heart longed for for my family.

In 2016 we created a family mission statement: we would open up our home and lives to other people. So my dream wasn't about a

specific home or drawing up designs
with an architect. It was having space
for people to come, learn, pray, grow,
be honest, rest, and maybe even take
a nap on my couch. I didn't need to

> Don't let your goals
> get in the way of where
> God is leading you now.

build a new home for that. I've found that most often when my
dreams don't work out it's because they don't actually center on
God. They focus on *me*. God sometimes lets me explore what He
knows will never wind up going anywhere. Ironically, God letting
us have our way for a time, when He knows He has something
better, can be a part of character refinement.

It is okay to want things we do not get—to have goals we do
not meet. Culture will tell us that unmet desire is unnecessary,
and we should do whatever it takes to meet it. The Bible tells us
unmet desire is necessary to hunger after God to feed it. ("I pray
to you, O LORD. I say, 'You are my place of refuge. You are all I
really want in life'" [Psalm 142:5 NLT].)

Ask the right questions.

To determine what should be pursued and what can be let
go, it's important to ask ourselves better questions than *What's
my dream?* Get more specific. Instead ask, *What does my heart long
for?* Remember, God wants to give us the desires of our hearts—
it's not wrong for our hearts to have longings. Because we also
know our hearts can lead us astray, it's important to pray, *God,
align the dreams in my heart to Yours* and to be in right relationship with Him, *first.* You don't want a dream God isn't a part of.
Those types of dreams never pan out.

Goals sometimes involve things like expectations, assumptions, optics, people pleasing, and comparison. Goals can be

awesome, but they don't automatically meet the longings of our hearts. Take your own inventory about this.

- Is someone's expectation of you driving what you think is a dream?
- Is your dream really an assumption of what you think you should be doing, achieving, or becoming?
- Does your dream feel important because it looks good on the outside and you long for the respect that comes with it?
- Have you told someone about this dream and feel like they will be disappointed in you or think less of you if you don't achieve it?
- Is it really your dream, or are you looking at where other people are or what they have, and is that driving you to pursue this particular dream?

Goals can be awesome, but they don't automatically meet the longings of our hearts.

Being honest with ourselves when we answer these questions is critical. We might have mislabeled things. For years we could have been calling what's really a *goal* motivated by the wrong reason a *dream* we wanted to come true.

Choosing to Let Dreams Live or Die

The inevitable next question after making the distinction between a goal and a dream: *When should I let a dream live and when should I let one die?*

The most important thing you need to answer I've already asked—*Is it a dream that supports and builds up the work of the kingdom of God?* As you narrow the lens and get into personal logistics, you can consider these things too: Do you sense this came from Him? Have you prayed through it and believe He is still in it? Is it something that supports your specific giftings and the call on your life? Does it continue to bring joy to you and those around you? Has your dream been affirmed by a solid spiritual mentor or influence in your life? Is your family and those who have your best interests at heart supportive of it? If the answer to these (or at least some of them) is yes, it is a dream that most likely deserves more life.

I'm not saying every dream must be an overtly spiritual one. Those that are less cut-and-dried will need to rely upon a solid relationship with Jesus for your decision-making. But while every dream doesn't have to have Bible verses attached to it, it should come under the umbrella of the commitment you've made to give Jesus your whole heart. It definitely can't be in conflict. Compartmentalized faith causes problems.

Here are my suggestions for dreams that need to die.

- Any dream that compromises your emotional, physical, or spiritual health and wellness.
- Any dream that is more about someone else's dream for you than your own.
- Any dream that makes you constantly feel competitive or unworthy.
- Any dream that leads you down destructive roads, changes you for the worse, or causes you to become unlike your created self.

- Any dream that godly, trusted family and friends don't support or believe is harming you.

Pay attention to these, because sometimes, we can't see what our dreams are actually doing to us. We think our dream is beautiful, but maybe other people have more perspective and see it's a bad relationship or endeavor. We might be sure something is a dream job, but maybe it's a work environment that will lead us down a dead-end road. I'm not suggesting we substitute someone else's judgment for our own—if our life belongs to Jesus, we have a biblical Spirit-guide for life. But we can't always see as clearly as the trusted friends around us who aren't as emotionally tied to a dream.

> Most of us don't quit on a real dream too soon. We live under the false hope of one too long.

And know that there are exceptions to every rule. Sometimes you might just have unsupportive friends. Sometimes a dream isn't what is causing your insecurity problems. Sometimes you need to hold on a little longer, and only God knows why it hasn't happened yet. Discouragement over waiting on a dream is what usually causes us to let it go too soon. Disappointment over broken dreams is what often causes us to stop dreaming, at least for a time. But most of us don't quit on a real dream too soon. We live under the false hope of one too long.

discouragement over waiting on a dream is what usually causes us to let it go too soon.

disappointment over broken dreams is what often causes us to stop dreaming, at least for a time.

What to Do While You're Waiting
for Your Dream to Happen

A young woman said something to me not long ago that I felt deep within my bones. "Why is it so hard to feel like I am ready for a dream that continues to not happen?" A strange mix of unwavering confidence and consistent humility is required to keep pursuing a dream.

She had the confidence her dream was the right one. The humility piece was what was so brutal; being denied over and over again when it doesn't happen can be hard to take. This is how we feel when we have a dream and have all the love, heart, passion, and possibly even qualifications to make it come true, but thus far, it has eluded us. It's difficult to see it continue not to happen, to say the least.

When we believe something is for us, it is hard to understand why it's not *happening* for us. But in both discouragement and disappointment, there is a covering of God's omniscience. He is certainly tender to our emotions, but His ultimate plan for us is unchanged. Therefore, in the scheme of life, nothing for us has, in fact, changed. Understanding what God is doing isn't a prerequisite to trust. Knowing what He is doing isn't even possible.

As you think very personally about your dreams, I want you to remember that because we are multifaceted people, the way you have processed the disappointment of some of your unrealized dreams has likely shown up in your body, even if you haven't considered this. God cares about how we responsibly exercise the

> Understanding what God is doing isn't a prerequisite to trust.

43

agency He has given us—to lean on His sufficiency even as we care for ourselves. In this process, please keep these four things in mind.

1. **Don't give up your dream simply because you're weary.** Some of the worst times to make big decisions are when we are worn down: hungry, tired, or mad about something else. Weariness is historically a time many lapses in judgment have been made and things that matter to us have been forgone in the name of over-whelm. Don't throw your dreams out the window just because you need a nap.

2. **Don't let fear keep you from taking the first step.** Doing it scared really does need to become a way of life. This is not to say we should settle for fear, because as overcomers in Christ, we are promised He can help us overcome it (and anything). But fear is also a human emotion that, in small measure, is even positive, or we would all do things like jump into active volcanoes and pick up rattlesnakes by their heads. Don't miss out on something great because fear makes it feel too enormous.

3. **Don't let assumption or bitterness creep in if God isn't working on your timetable.** Candidly, patience is no one's real strong suit. None of us wants to wait on a dream. The tendency in the lull periods of life (especially when we desire something not happening quickly enough) is to go to assumption or bitterness. Resist both of those things. Don't assume you know what God's doing because He isn't doing it your way.

4. **Don't ask other people's permission to fulfill the dreams God has for you.** Your dreams may affect others, but they are between you and God. Live them wisely. Make sure they are right. But stop taking endless polls from others about what they think God wants you to do. Trust your relationship with Him. Don't ask for the rights to dreams from people they don't belong to.

Ultimately, from the beginning, our dreams all belong to God. It's such a privilege to get to be alive, to get to dream and see many of our dreams happen. And even when they don't? They were still beautiful to have for a time, weren't they?

God knows what we crave, those private dreams, and the things that feel just out of our reach. He cares about them. All of it matters. He has our big picture in mind. We need to be encouraged by our dreaming. It's a sign of life.

Understanding the Dream-Giver is really the most important thing here. Our dreams don't exist without Him because our lives do not exist without Him. I hope that your understanding about God's good and thorough knowledge of your life—from breath to burial—will encourage you to remember that there is no setback, broken dream, or far-off desire that God doesn't want to be a part of redeeming.

I understand that God can feel far when we are dreaming,

> God knows what we crave, those private dreams, and the things that feel just out of our reach. He cares about them. All of it matters. He has our big picture in mind. We need to be encouraged by our dreaming. It's a sign of life.

especially when the dream feels out of reach. The dream may, in turn, become simply for God to not feel far.

I can assure you, He is not.

Paul gives some incredible imagery in Acts 17 to help illustrate this.

> From one man he made all the nations, that they should inhabit the whole earth; and he marked out their appointed times in history and the boundaries of their lands. God did this so that they would seek him and perhaps reach out for him and find him, though he is not far from any one of us. "For in him we live and move and have our being." As some of your own poets have said, "We are his offspring." (Acts 17:26–28)

Even in the midst of our darkness as we are reaching out, even as we navigate through the darkness of our dreams, God is not far. Imagine it like being in a room where you can't see your hand in front of your face; you have your hand out in front of you, waving it around, trying to maneuver around the obstacles to find your way out. You have dreams you can't see your way into or out of—goals and plans and things you desperately want to work out in your heart. At times you feel at a loss, as if you are engulfed in a dark room of what you believe and hope and it's all with limited vision. And often, you are. Often in our dreams we are in darkness. And in that same space, God is always meeting us there.

He isn't the door holder; He's the Door.

He isn't tacked onto the end of our dreams; He *is* the dream.

Because God knows my dreams, I can find safety in renewing them.

Renew: 3 Steps to Move Forward

1. Take a nap. As silly as this may sound, a lot of dreams have gotten thrown out the window because we were tired. Rest is crucial in discernment about your dreams because it helps calibrate emotions.

2. Organize your dream into bite-sized pieces. Make a dream timeline, working your way back. Even though we make plans, God determines the steps. Write a date you'd love to see it come to fruition, then rewind. While factoring in rest, include time for mentorship/accountability "stops" and tasks that may need to get done.

3. Keep a prayer journal about your dreams and goals. Ask God to help you discern one from the other. Begin to separate what are dreams, God dreams, and perhaps prophetic dreams.

God Knows the Vindication You Seek

If it is possible, as far as it depends on you, live at peace
with everyone. Do not take revenge, my dear friends,
but leave room for God's wrath, for it is written: "It
is mine to avenge; I will repay," says the Lord.

Romans 12:18–19

I was eighteen years old around the time rumors were passing through the grapevine about my father's potential affair, which for a pastor of a church is of particular concern. Not only did I, as his daughter, want to disbelieve it, but I felt passionate to defend our family name after time and again hearing it come out of someone's mouth—often with at least some element of falsehood. Hurt, weary, fiercely loyal (and in a particular *hold-my-earrings* season of life after also dealing with some painful mean-girl harassment), I was in peak vindication mode when I was told the name of a person I knew who was the source behind several of the most damaging rumors about my dad. That day, I was done with victimhood. I was over people saying things that weren't true and causing my family pain. I was through with doing "the right thing" by staying silent. In my mind, this had to stop, and I was the one to stop it.

Personal confrontation, biblically speaking, wouldn't have been the wrong approach. Matthew 18 teaches us to go directly to someone who has wronged us. But I was mad. I wasn't seeking spiritual reconciliation; I was seeking to feel better through my own form of vengeance. Those things change the game.

To make matters more combustible, I would be confronting this person at work, in a busy public place. So the conditions weren't appropriate. In a fog of anger and teenage reasoning, I did not consider this to be of concern.

It's been more than thirty years, but I can still remember whipping into the parking lot, jerking the car into park. The warm summer air enveloped me as I stepped out of the car and slammed the door, and the cold air hit me as I stormed into the store in what seemed like less than ten steps. I walked fast so I didn't lose my courage. I can remember the exact moment of confrontation—walking straight up to where this person stood, working, without regard to my foolishness, and giving this person a piece of my mind. I can feel the heat rising to my ears and the adrenaline coursing through my entire body and the way my heel turned to walk away when I finished saying what I wanted to say, without waiting on a response.

I did it: approached the one who had hurt my family. Did I feel better? I wasn't sure yet. I walked outside and slid behind the driver's seat, heart beating fast and hands shaking.

My father sure wasn't impressed by my theatrics. I found that out quickly thereafter, when I drove to his office and someone had already let him know. (Small-town grapevine, again, thanks.) "You can't go around chewing out everyone who starts a rumor, Lisa," he said, "or you'll have a full-time job." I knew I couldn't, but my desire to set the record straight had caused me to at least try.

That wasn't the last rumor that was started about my family. Some were true, some were false, and some were somewhere in the middle, as rumors usually are. Some stories were crueler and hurt deeper, and some I've never written about. But Daddy was right. I could never fight them all, even though I wanted to. The desire to get peace for the pain other people caused often felt overwhelming. In the days that followed, my revenge-seeking was a symptom of something deeper: I felt helpless. Then I felt afraid. Angry. And then I tried to control it.

Seeking vindication over something like gossip certainly didn't feel small to me at the time, when gossip was hurting and affecting my family. And gossip isn't a small concern when you consider how it damages people. I've seen people lose jobs, opportunities, relationships, ministries, and even their lives. James calling gossip a fire in James 3 is wildly accurate. The damage gossip can do—even when there is some truth to the rumor—is not minor.

"Consider what a great forest is set on fire by a small spark. The tongue also is a fire, a world of evil among the parts of the body. It corrupts the whole body, sets the whole course of one's life on fire, and is itself set on fire by hell" (James 3:5–6).

But both things can be true:

> Gossip isn't a small concern when you consider how it damages people.

gossip is wrong, *and* we can also be wrong in how we go about trying to vindicate it. This is the case with vengeance regardless of the issue; it is different from biblical confrontation and different from advocacy for biblical justice. God's omniscience covers the wrongs done to you that you long to personally make right. He knows what happened, knows the truth, and in one way or another, will set it straight.

> **biblical confrontation**: Motivated by reconciliation, not self-interest—follows the guideline from Scripture: "If your brother sins against you, go tell him his fault, between you and him alone. If he listens to you, you have won your brother. But if he won't listen, take one or two others with you, so that by the testimony of two or three witnesses every fact may be established. If he doesn't pay attention to them, tell the church. If he doesn't pay attention even to the church, let him be like a Gentile and a tax collector to you."(Matthew 18:15–17 csb)

The Illusion of Payback

When you're fighting hard to defend yourself, you're trying to throw your hot potato of pain into someone else's hands. They might catch it, but it's still your potato.

What most of us want to do is pay someone back for what they have done to us—transfer to them the feelings of helplessness, sorrow, anger, and insecurity we felt when they inflicted pain on us. But what's it really about? Getting out of pain. If transferring our discomfort to them would do it, it might be a harder sell on asking us not to try to get even. But payback is an illusion, and any of us who have tried to pay someone back for the hurt they have caused us know this full well.

Payback-Seeking Pattern

Feel helpless

Feel afraid

Feel angry

Try to control it

copyright Lisa Whittle

When I gave the person who started the rumor about my father a piece of my mind at their work, I wanted them to feel low—lower than I felt for the rumors they had been telling. But if I had been able to discern what I was actually dealing with, I'd have known it was much more. My heart was wounded from people who I thought loved our family not being there when we needed them the most. I was weary from the effort of squashing lies. I was dealing with my own questions and issues of faith and my fears of my father not being who he said he was. But I didn't want to deal with any of that. It was easier to throw that hot potato into the other person's hands to have to deal with.

But it doesn't work that way. Our attempts at paying people back do not take away the issue at hand. In many cases, they just give us another issue. After my visit to the rumor-starter's work, I was now juggling an additional hot potato—having to answer to my father, face the whispers that were now making their way through the grapevine about what I had done, and deal with the Lord. It wasn't too long after the confrontation that the Holy Spirit began convicting me about my actions. Trying to pay people back never eases the pain of what they've done to us. It only extends it.

Is there a wrong you are trying to make right by seeking payback?

What do you hope to gain from it?

The best way to seek vindication is to let God, who is fully aware of the situation, heal you from it. His healing will be more thorough because He knows what you know *and more*. In this relationship of intimacy, your pain lessens as your relationship of trust with Jesus grows. This is how people truly become better instead of bitter—God loves them through that process. There is no story as powerful as the one of someone who has committed to stay engaged in a life that has not been fair to them. Fighting for anything makes the end result that much more meaningful. But only God makes that possible. Once we trust Him enough to do the fighting for us, we will emerge from our victimhood.

The easy way out is to stay angry and vengeful. It's the quick and natural response. When not confronted, it will stick around. But it isn't the way to have a good life. There is nothing sadder than when someone lets years of living with a chip on their shoulder take their potential away. Conversely, there is nothing stronger than a person who hasn't let other people's actions toward them turn them bitter and unloving. It takes a lot of Jesus to stop wanting to pay someone back. He is crucial to this equation. If He is handling the business of injustice, globally and personally, He can surely help us move forward despite how the actions of others have threatened to hinder us.

> The best way to seek vindication is to let God, who is fully aware of the situation, heal you from it.

biblical justice: alignment with God's plan for justice/pursuing kingdom causes, even if it's of personal cost to us; motive is not rooted in self, but in our commitment to follow Christ.

I realize we can know these things and even believe them and have the desire to live them out. But often, the emotions of the desired revenge cause us to overrule what we know. In these moments when emotions feel especially pressing, here are some practical things to do—I call them the Three Ps before you get payback: *pause, pray,* and *ponder.*

1. **Pause:** Often, it is our quick reactions that get us in the most trouble. Pausing helps give us distance from the intensity of a situation and clarity on how we should respond. Even a five-second pause can make a difference. (Remember the age-old advice to count to ten?)

2. **Pray:** The greatest help we ever get is from God. He knows the ins and outs of our situation. Praying is the key to getting results in your life.

3. **Ponder:** Think through your next steps. Write them down. When you consider your movement, you will be much more purposeful about it. A plan can often save you from regret from a hasty payback.

Had I taken my own advice and done these things before I confronted the person starting rumors about my family, I would definitely have done things differently. I didn't pray about it. I didn't think about it. I didn't hesitate to get in my car and drive over the minute I heard news of a new rumor. Though things had been accumulating, there was no urgency for me to take it into my own hands. Only in my mind did I need to try to make it stop that very day.

As you implement the third part of this Three-P system, here are a few practical things for you to consider before you try to pay someone back.

Temporary payback isn't the same as true benefit.

Easy often equals empty. There's a difference between a Band-Aid and a salve. A Band-Aid will be the result of our lashing out or attempting to pay someone back—a temporary quick fix. It often not only will not have the results we want—it won't heal like a salve—but it won't be as satisfying as we think. It reminds me of all those cartoons I watched every Saturday morning, with the coyote manically setting traps to take down the roadrunner. Without fail, the traps would always backfire on the coyote and wind up hurting him instead. We think we want to pay people back, but it never really benefits us in the way we imagine it will. Because God never intended for us to do His job.

Quick revenge robs us of correct perspective.

We can go rogue when we feel like it, but it will delay our ability to deal rightly with injustice, even from a right viewpoint. When we seek out a human form of justice, though this seems like an offensive strategy, we are coming from a posture of defense—we are trying to right wrongs. Defensiveness cannot drive a wise process. Every decision will be made from feelings of resentment. Most of all, we will be denying the omniscience of God—that He knows about the wrong we long to make right and, in that knowledge, is actively working in and through it.

We will never do as thorough a job as God.

Unless we believe we are equal to God, we have to know that everything we do, including using human methods to pay someone back for a wrong done to us, will not be done as well as He'd do it. We may want it done quicker, or in our way, but if we want it done *best* we will let Him handle it. Paying people back doesn't bring peace of mind. It might bring some temporary satisfaction, but so do a lot of things that aren't good for us.

Vengeance Versus Vindication

In times of hurt, emotions can run high. This is why knowing the difference between vengeance and vindication is important. Vengeance is about *pursuing revenge at all costs and using our preferred methods*. Vindication is *a natural desire to have our name cleared, a wrong made right, the record to be set straight*. It is a normal human emotion to want our name to be cleared or defended. None of us wants to feel like we are being wrongly accused of something, nor do we want someone who hurt us to get away with it. But vindication is far less about us than we may even truly understand. Consider Romans 12:18–20:

> If it is possible, as far as it depends on you, live at peace with everyone. Do not take revenge, my dear friends, but leave room for God's wrath, for it is written: "It is mine to avenge; I will repay," says the Lord. On the contrary: "If your enemy is hungry, feed him; if he is thirsty, give him something to drink. In doing this, you will heap burning coals on his head."

Paul was writing to the Romans about the personal responsibility we have in living as a sacrifice *to God*. So even as Paul was giving this illustration, which we're using to discuss aspects of human relationships such as peace and payback, Jesus was calling us to community with *Himself,* the God who is fully aware of the entire situation. This, again, is why focusing on the bigger picture of God and His omniscience, instead of ourselves, is important. It is the key to helping us live at peace with people rather than the self-help methods we have attempted so far.

We have already been wounded by someone when we experience a perceived injustice; what we cannot afford, in our attempts toward revenge, is a fracturing of our relationship with the God who is eager to help us. It's not that God would remove help to spite us in our attempts to vindicate ourselves, but in the sovereign order of help, we are refusing the benefit. Creating unnecessary distance. It is as if we are saying to God, "Thank You, but I do not need Your help." This attitude of autonomy has historically gotten every believer embroiled in their own turmoil and trouble. We create complications by involving ourselves with temporary methods that not only do not satisfy but often cause greater angst. And, too, we are withholding our true vindication and relief.

> What we cannot afford, in our attempts toward revenge, is a fracturing of our relationship with the God who is eager to help us.

Paul was promoting, in this passage, resolution as a first resort— yes, even with those who may not deserve it. He was saying to trust God to do the job you so desperately want to handle. He was suggesting that a kind response to someone who has wronged you is a far smarter strategy, and works much better. And when he said to "leave room for God's wrath" he was assuring us justice *will* come. It just may not be on our timetable.

While I'll dive into this more at the end of the chapter, I want to make it clear what I am *not* saying:

- **I am not saying to never seek justice.** There are absolutely times for that, even for less cut-and-dried biblical matters.
- **I am not saying all injustice is created equal.** There is a difference between seeking biblical justice and seeking vengeance.
- **I am not saying victims of abuse should seek resolution.** Please consult a professional (counselor, law enforcement, etc.) in cases where abuse is present. Physical/sexual abuse

victims should never seek resolution or accept meetings with an abuser. Spiritual-abuse victims should also not meet with their abusers alone, at the very least.

When we feel that someone has been unfair to us, we feel in some way victimized, so the natural tendency is to turn to a control approach to take the power back. The pattern often looks like this:

Unhealthy Approach to Things That Feel Unfair

Incident occurs

Feeling arises
(natural responses to a feeling of a lack of ability to control what happened)

Action is taken
(trying to take power back by taking matters into your own hands)

Lingering pain
(action was unsatisfactory—results in fear, resentment/bitterness for what you are unable to change or make right and your belief you should, can, or still want to)

copyright Lisa Whittle

But there is a better way. We can't control what other people do, nor can we control the natural feelings that arise when things that hurt us happen, but we do have positive choice in the matter from there.

Healthy Approach to Things That Feel Unfair

Incident occurs

↓

Feeling arises
(natural responses to a feeling of a lack of ability to control what happened)

↓

Positive choice
1. Remembrance—Ask yourself "What do I know to be true about God?"
2. Identity Check—Read Psalm 139 to remind yourself of who you are.
3. Surrender—Best surrender method: prayer. As we surrender our inability to control what has or might happen over to God, we are better able to cope.

↓

Follow up
(Healthy repetition is the best way to continue a lifestyle of better coping methods. Repetition is a spiritual practice—we repeat good, God things to get better. Repeat this new approach, over and over again.)

copyright Lisa Whittle

Vengeance is never the way. Vindication is God's way, and we can trust Him to bring it in His time and within His parameters.

Things We Wish Were True but Aren't

At some point, unfair treatment happens to us all, though not equally. Please hear me say that—there is not a one-size-fits-all justice/injustice scale in this world. It is simply, like everything earthly, imbalanced. It's reasonable to ask people who don't share our same experiences to become more empathetic, but it is unreasonable to expect them to be humanly able to wear our skin. People can listen to us, but they cannot fully know. They can respond on our behalf to injustices, but they will be doing so out of a secondhand understanding. It is insincere to suggest otherwise. This built-in imbalance excuses no one of responsibility—the evergreen responsibility we have to do right, love mercy, and walk humbly before our God (Micah 6:8). This right-doing most certainly involves how we advocate for others. But understanding our limitations as a secondhand party to someone else's injustices helps us give grace in each other's imperfection and perhaps even their stumbling along the way of trying to empathize with us. The intentions in our actions must count for something—otherwise, we will never allow anyone to love us through mistakes. I wish we would always get it right, but we won't. I wish we were able to fully understand everyone's situation, but we are not. But there is a way through this. God's omniscience bridges the gap: the Holy Spirit gives us intuition, tenderness, and protectiveness toward people He *does* know all things about. It is a holy transfer of His spirit of justice.

Faulty thinking about what is just and what is unjust is what causes us to crawl into a hole we struggle to get out of when something doesn't line up for us. Our world has started to carry the tone that everything is an injustice, and when that happens, nothing is. True injustices risk our callousness, where many of us are just so tired of hearing people screaming foul at every turn. We become hardened to the true injustices (and histrionic over the things we simply don't feel willing to entrust to God). The trouble is, there are things worth screaming about. In some cases, the screaming should be louder. This is why the world shouldn't be leading the charge for justice—the church should be. But for the church to do so, we have to stop our cowardice and step up. In the past, the church hasn't been willing to see justice issues as gospel issues because of our shallow, one-note faith. Also, our fear. It is a farce that we cannot stay true to convictions and reconsider the way we once were taught to execute our faith. We can love God and the Bible and extend our pro-life beliefs to more than just anti-abortion. We can love God and the Bible and advocate for the poor. We can love God and the Bible and question both political parties. In fact, we should do all those things. There is no conservative and progressive when it comes to the kingdom of God. There is Jesus, the cross, salvation, and making disciples. Loving people isn't code for losing biblical footing. Believing the Bible isn't code for legalism. It's time to stop being so self-centered and focus on following the example of Jesus instead.

Out of all the complications, the one thing that unites us is our humanity: our desire for a neat and tidy, linear rightness that funnels people into doing the right thing *and* our true need for God who will actually do the right thing for us. Often, He will be the only One. The rumors about my father were far from the last time someone wronged me. Many of those other moments, and their details, I've kept silent for years—some involving churches, ministry leadership, friends, loved ones. I'm not telling you that's a choice *you* should always make. We must all depend on the Holy Spirit for this individual guidance. (Abuse, again, should never be kept quiet.) I only know that in my situation, the times God has specifically prompted me to stay silent have been hard. But they have also been surprisingly *good*. In our quiet

There is no conservative and progressive when it comes to the kingdom of God.

In our quiet consecration to God, He has the ability to speak healing over our unspoken wrongs.

consecration to God, He has the ability to speak healing over our unspoken wrongs. This will be a more satisfying vindicator. In those places of mine He has privately healed, I need no further closure.

God's omniscience has been the single factor that prompted me to speak or stay silent. In my flesh, I wouldn't have known which was the right move. In the end, anytime God has guided me to close my mouth about something someone did to me, I have learned (and relearned) to live without other people handing me peace that only God could truly give me. This is an incredible perk—a breakthrough for many of us with people pleasing. Along the way it may be a bumpy ride, but stick with it. If you are facing a moment like this and you wonder, *Will I be able to live without telling my side of the story?* I want you to know it is enough to have been right and only you and God ever knew it. Maybe not today, but as you give it to Him, you *will* get there. God may vindicate you quickly, or maybe not in this lifetime. But what you really want is something we all want: more than to be right, to be able to live without needing the justice we once thought we couldn't live without. Vindication doesn't feel

Vindication doesn't feel as good as we hope. Not needing it feels better.

as good as we hope. Not needing it feels better.

You are not alone in your struggle with this. I'm going to help you with some tangible new coping methods you can use in the future when injustices happen—since we know they will. But sometimes we struggle because we hold on to false hopes and beliefs about something, and I want to clear up a few "faulty *ifs*" about injustices that may come our way so we can move forward with a healthier outlook.

Faulty *If* 1: If I do right, things will go right for me.

If only this were true, we who follow programs, formulas, and recipes—who know how to live by rules and systems—would be in excellent shape. If doing right were the key to preventing wrongs, wouldn't all the saints be winners and all the sinners be losers? We already know the world's justice system isn't fair. And, since we are all sinners, that messes up the hope of getting off on good behavior. We've seen "good people" have things go desperately wrong. They followed the formulas but faced terrible tragedy. How can I explain it? The short answer: I cannot.

In situations like this, injustices cause us to question our faith. Because if God is really good then why wouldn't He honor right living? If the Bible tells us how to live and we do our best to meet that standard, shouldn't we be immune to heartache? These are not bad questions. Even with our kids, it's hard to explain where God was in an unfair process—for things that are not cruel injustices but often feel unjust when they have worked hard at something, behaved like they were told, are "good kids," and things didn't always go as they planned. We teach them that if they put in hard work out on the field, they will be rewarded with a spot on the team. Or if they work hard in the classroom, they will be in the top tier of their class or get a scholarship. Knowing that life is unpredictable, we tell them there is no guarantee so they won't be disappointed if it doesn't happen. Yet we, ourselves, wrestle with the unfairness when the work they put in doesn't equal payoff. Have you been to a high school sports event lately? Watch the aggression of the parents in the stands. Ask a coach how parents take to their child not getting playing time or getting benched.

And it *is* hard when our child has done the right thing, or we have done the right thing in life, and the rug is pulled out from under us. It's hard when people do us wrong. It's hard to explain injustice to our children, especially since we often don't understand it.

This is a natural human feeling. Sometimes the ache of no explanation is the hardest thing for us to endure. But we also have to consider that in some way, we may not have the full and correct picture of God. If we have relegated God to the vending machine who pays out for our good behavior, we will present Him that way—even subtly—to our kids. If we consider His knowledge to be incomplete or in any way biased, we will diminish its importance. The benefit of God's omniscience to us requires trust in its reliability. It is no wonder behavior modification is more valued in many faith communities than true heart change. We think God is judging us like we judge each other, and we base gifts on short-term reward systems instead of the long game of sanctification that God is all about.

To become realigned with the truth, it's important for us to understand that our "goodness" isn't a bar for blessing (that is beneficial to us, since that would require God to be partial and us to live a life dependent upon good works, which would equal exhaustion), just as our "goodness" does not exclude us from the world's injustice. That is merely a consequence of living in a fallen world. (Jesus said, "In this world you will have trouble" [John 16:33].) Likewise, the justice we receive for our wrongdoing does not mean God is not good. His character doesn't change because of human behavior. Our assessment of personal worthiness isn't factored into God's knowledge of situations. Romans 3:10 reminds us: "As it is written: 'None is righteous, no, not one'" (ESV). So we don't get to decide the shoulds and shouldn'ts of goodness and God.

God knowing what is best for us does not include winners and losers. That is not how God works. He doesn't rob one person of a blessing to give it to someone else.

What is true is that sometimes we will *do* right and it will not *go* right for us. That is not because God is not good or we have done wrong. It is because the world is not good, and until God returns to take us to a perfect heaven, things will be imperfect.

Faulty *If* 2: If I am kind, people will behave kindly toward me.

The Golden Rule was perfect, once again, for behavior modification for us as children, but we were sold it as a promise of guaranteed reciprocation. This led to our great letdown when we found out it wasn't always the case. We still get disappointed when we are kind or generous to others and they do not return the favor—often indignantly so, if not offended. Our perception based on the Golden Rule idea is that people will match our behavior; therefore, we can predetermine our emotional fate in this world, at least in relationships. Wouldn't that be nice, if we could control that?

We can control ourselves in it, but that's all. Every one of us approaches relationships with preferences, biases, baggage, and history, and few of us can overcome those things enough to have healthy long-term relationships—we've proven that. We certainly can't do it without God. Long-running friendships are rare. Long-running marriages too. Kids and parents and siblings still speaking to each other when everyone grows up. There are many factors that lead to our fractures, but people are unpredictable and can withdraw from us without our consent. Many have. I have experienced it and heard from many of you who live in pain over wishing you could bring a loved one back.

We aren't perfect, and often we have in some way contributed to our own pain. Sometimes, though, we truly have not. And yes, we should do unto others as we would want them to do unto us, but with the understanding they may not. What if we are kind and they aren't kind back? What if we are a good friend and they are a lousy one? What if we are honest with them and they lie to us?

These things can and do happen. The kindness we exercise toward others is still right. Honesty is still the best choice. But none of us behaves perfectly. Put the camera on our lives and we would all be embarrassed about something.

Sometimes someone is actively hurtful to us. We invested in them only to have them break our hearts. I went through a friendship breakup several years ago, and it was particularly difficult because of what I'd poured into her. No one was completely faultless in the situation, including me. But she did some things that were blatantly wrong. My only consolation was that God knew, and eventually, when unjust things in the past like this have happened to me or my family, the truth came out. It's different when God manages our PR rather than us trying to do it ourselves. His knowledge of our situation brings a protective factor that has a way of bringing false information to light.

You've been through the same or similar. Sometimes people will be biased against us, and we can do nothing about it. Sometimes they will be jealous. Sometimes they will be cruel. Our job is not to try to change people's minds. It is to simply keep doing what God has called us to do and let Him work it out on our behalf. ("The LORD will fight for you; you need only to be still" [Exodus 14:14].) Apologies have come to me after wrongdoing, and I have given them out to others because God's prompting through conviction is always the best reconciler. If either party had tried to force it, it would have never happened. Even if that redemption day doesn't come, it is not for a lack of God working.

His knowledge of our situation brings a protective factor that has a way of bringing false information to light.

Things like this can be important lessons for us—injustices can be our teacher. They hurt, but they can also help us be more careful with our own stories in the future—both those we tell and those we are willing to hear about someone else. What if what you heard about someone was wrong and you wasted a long time believing it? What if you prevented God's work in someone's life because you biased someone against them, or prevented God's work in *your* life because *you* were biased and did not treat His child with love and kindness?

You might be a good friend to someone, and they aren't a good friend back.

You might be honest, and someone cheats you.

You might be kind, and someone responds in anger.

Their response is not your responsibility. But you are still responsible to do right.

Honestly, the general distrust a lot of us live with these days comes naturally, but many times it also comes *from* somewhere.

Most of us didn't start out distrustful; babies are the most trusting humans in the world. But life has the tendency to try to crush the trust out of us. It wants to jade us. We can become prickly, with our heads on a swivel, daring people to be true. A lot of us once trusted, but something happened that changed our minds. Unfair treatment, even small incidents through the years, can pile up and eventually cause us to shut down or severely alter course.

I had a conversation with a young woman recently who was struggling in her marriage after her husband began saying he was no longer a believer in Jesus and had a desire to explore other religions. Their marriage was young, and their background was deeply rooted in the church; in fact, they had served in church leadership positions. On instinct, I asked her if they had a bad work experience in ministry. She said they had, and in fact her husband had been treated quite unfairly, and it had caused him a lot of pain. I knew what was likely going on because it is the story of many: the actions of people who professed Jesus as their Lord had been so egregious, it had led to a broken trust in this man's faith in God. It was no surprise he was searching. The pain from the experience while doing the Lord's work was sadly connected, and everything that came after, until that wound was healed, would make it hard to trust God.

That's why we bear such responsibility in our actions; the way we treat each other marks the name of Jesus. Despite the fact that we must look to God and not each other for perfection, human beings' poor behavior affects how we feel about a supernatural God who is not to blame. Being a follower of Jesus doesn't mean we are automatically following Him well.

Blind trust is never wise, nor am I suggesting it. All throughout the New Testament there are qualifications and expectations for Christians who live together in community. Intimate community is possible because of trust, and trust comes from verified believable behavior over time. Even trusting God without any qualifications isn't blind trust, because we have seen and know who He is, so our belief in Him is not without proof. We have proof that God can be trusted. People can't reach His level, but we can all follow His example. People show us who they are and how they are willing to be for us, in order for us to offer them our trust. Loving people is not the same as trusting them in the sense

> Being a follower of Jesus doesn't mean we are automatically following Him well.

that we open up our deepest heart-needs to just anyone. (Enter, boundaries!) At the same time, we shouldn't distrust people automatically. Once again, it is the tension of living in both with the help of Christ. And if you think you can go through life not trusting anyone? It's not true. Trust me, I've tried.

This is where God, once again, must be the center. Do you trust *Him* in all of this? That is the real question.

What *Is* True: God Is Love, God Is Just, and We Can Trust

God's love and justice are a complete set. His omniscience—the fact that He knows about everything happening in the world and in our lives—gives Him the awareness of every unjust thing that is going on, both globally and in every personal feeling of unfair treatment. Out of His love for us, He can exercise the power to make it right. We won't understand the timing and methods around this because we do not have His mind. But it doesn't negate the truth of it. It is, though, why we often struggle when we see injustices happening or feel we are the ones who have been wronged. These may be on different scales of intensity and true injustice, but our feelings about God in them are often the same or similar. To us, it *appears* God is either absent or calloused. He is neither, but in order to believe that, we must believe He loves us without bias or condition, and out of that love He is both able and intentional in how He will go about making good on His promise to rectify our situation. If we have a difficult time with this, we may not truly believe God's unconditional love for us. Or we may be dealing with an issue of self, wanting control. Or we may disbelieve God is truly just. Or, for a time, we may just be angry. That is real too. Please believe that God is more than capable of being the kind God who loves you thoroughly and, equally, the just God who fights for you fiercely, and at the same time, will be just in how He approaches your sin. This is how His love and justice are perfectly intertwined.

Often, our belief about God's intention toward justice involves how we feel about His timing. Timing is what trips us up a lot—pain goes on too long for our liking, and we become doubters and wanderers anew. Psalm 75:2–3 speaks to God's intimate and thorough timing, "'At the time I have planned, I will bring justice against the wicked. When the earth quakes and its people live in turmoil, I am the one who keeps its foundations firm'" (NLT). Don't ever doubt: He is in absolute control.

God's justice involves His timing, whether or not we like it. His is the correct timing because He has something we don't— perfect knowledge, knowing exactly when the right and perfect time is. In the New Testament, kairos means "the appointed time in the purpose of God," the time when God acts. ("'The time has come,' he said. 'The kingdom of God has come near. Repent and believe the good news!'" [Mark 1:15].) "Time" and "appointed time" in Scripture often refer to the end of time—this means in many instances, we will not see justice on this earth. But does that mean God does not love us? Absolutely not. His love does not change. It simply means that our inability to know what He does prevents us from understanding justice—God's thorough, perfect, right-timed moment to set things right.

The sixty-six-chapter book of Isaiah is not only one of my favorites in the Bible, but it is also a book that beautifully illustrates both the love and the justice of God. If you read it without knowing that it is basically split into two parts (some scholars split it into three), it might be very confusing. *Is God cruel or good? Is He loving or condemning?* The answer is: He is loving *and* He is just.

The first part of Isaiah is often called First Isaiah (chapters 1–39), the second Deutero-Isaiah (chapters 40–55 or 40–66), and the third—if the second section is subdivided—Trito-Isaiah (chapters 56–66).[1] When you read chapters 1–39, you'll find pockets of reprieve among a message of judgment over the sins of Israel and Judah. Some beautiful promises of restoration, calls to trust the Lord, and of course, the greatest prophetic message of comfort in the entire Bible in Isaiah 9, which foretells of the coming Messiah: "For a child is born to us, a son is given to us. The government will rest on his shoulders. And he will be called: Wonderful Counselor, Mighty God, Everlasting Father, Prince of Peace. His government and its peace will never end. He will rule with fairness and justice from the throne of his ancestor David for all eternity" (vv. 6–7 NLT). Justice in these thirty-nine chapters flows from the pen of most likely the prophet Isaiah himself.

Chapters 40–66, however, take a noticeably different tone (one reason many believe these chapters may have been written by another author). Messages of help, salvation, hope, deliverance, and blessing give us the good news found here. Love is the underlying theme. God seeing and knowing and bringing everything full circle to make it right.

It is the message of the gospel—the message of our lives. God is good, He loves us, and He will bring what is undone to completion, both in us and in this world—what is right and what is not right.

Isaiah 5:15–16 says: "Humanity will be destroyed, and people brought down; even the arrogant will lower their eyes in humiliation. But the LORD of Heaven's Armies will be exalted by his justice. The holiness of God will be displayed by his righteousness" (NLT). Often, when we read the Bible we think of all the ways God will make it right on our behalf. But the Bible is about God, not about us. His justice is about making it right on behalf *of the kingdom of God.* As He brings justice to the world and even our world, He is doing so out of love for us, yes, but with a bigger picture than we would imagine. His justice is big, just as is His omniscience. And so it is not for us to ever fully wrap our minds around. It is for us to trust, to believe, and to cling to when the world's injustice affects us personally. At some point for all of us, it will.

Friend, God's omniscience has to be true, or *nothing is true.*

The injustice in this world may be the single most important reason we need to believe God's omniscience to be able to keep going.

God is good, He loves us, and
He will bring what is undone
to completion, both in us and
in this world—what is right
and what is not right.

God is good, He

He will bring wh

to completion, b

All the things we say we believe, all the things we cling to in the darkest night, the entire message that keeps us hopeful—if God doesn't know about the things that are wrong in our lives, we cannot be assured they will ever be made right.

But if it's true that God knows everything, we have a solution to the soul distress we feel when we release both the world's travesties and our personal desires for vindication over to God. We can trust Him with our worries and whys. And because of that, we can be comforted and relieved from our everyday methods of trying to control, manage, change, and help them.

I know there are things happening in so many of our lives that we don't like the looks of. I struggle with these same things. But I have come to the conclusion that I would rather believe in God in unjust situations than live with the greater pain that I have nothing to believe in at all. Because the hope that comes from the idea that there is redemption I don't know of in the end, helps me go on. And with God, it will be perfect. Turning away from God in our pain is only taking our greatest relief away from us. We can be confused and even angry with God for a time and still get relief from trusting in Him if we keep faith alive. The Christian life is, more than anything, a life of great paradox. We are living while we are dying, and we are trusting while we daily battle doubt.

> The injustice in this world may be the single most important reason we need to believe God's omniscience to be able to keep going.

Don't go through life holding your breath, hoping someone won't hurt you. They might, but that's no way to live. If they do, God will be there to help you.

Don't put all your faith in another human who isn't capable of being perfect. They will be a huge letdown. God won't.

Allow someone the opportunity to keep their word. What if they do? And if they don't, God will.

And please, above all else, don't let the injustices that have broken your trust in the past change the person you are. Rudeness and woundedness are often the same person in different clothes. Bitterness often has a backstory.

The desire for vindication loves to stay in its cycles. And God wants to break them all.

Because God knows about my life, I trust Him to rectify that which I can't make right.

Rectify: 3 Steps to Move Forward

1. Name an experience you want vindication for and write it down somewhere—either in your phone notes, in a journal, or even just on a piece of paper. Does it have to do with a person, a system, a group of people, a specific situation, or even God? Look at the payback pattern and see if you followed it, and, if so, where you think it went negatively for you.

2. Evaluate your thoughts about revenge before you read this chapter and now after. How does a biblical perspective help you know better what to pursue and how to pursue it?

3. Consider the unhealthy approach to seeking payback and the healthy approach. Use your new approach on unjust situations moving forward as they arise.

Helps for Biblical Justice Seeking

- **Start with biblical understanding.** Biblical justice seeking is, at its core, *ambassadorship*. Second Corinthians 5:20 says we are ambassadors of Christ: "So we are Christ's ambassadors; God is making his appeal through us. We speak for Christ when we plead, 'Come back to God!'" (NLT). *Presbeutēs*, the Greek word for "ambassador," means, broadly, "to function as a representative of a ruling authority."[1] To be an ambassador in the ancient world (Greek, Roman, or Jewish), as in modern times, involved three things: (1) a commissioning for a special assignment; (2) representing the sender; and (3) exercising the authority of the sender. Seeking godly justice, done as His ambassador, will have the same characteristics. We represent Him for a special assignment. We seek to advocate for a kingdom cause, under His authority.

- **Check the signs and motives.** Biblical justice seeking is activism compelled by a love for Christ. It shouldn't be hard to recognize. There will be love, even in the boldness. There will be peace, even in the assertiveness. There will be joy, even in the difficulty. There will be truth in the midst of confusion and steadiness in the midst of turmoil. Jesus was out of the box, but He did not do things haphazardly. There was no duplicity in His reason for seeking justice. He had one mission: the kingdom of God. This, too, will be our mission.

- **Ask questions.**
  1. Is someone in need of an advocate? **"Defend the weak and the fatherless; uphold the cause of the poor and the oppressed"** (Psalm 82:3–4).
  2. Is someone facing personal harm or lack? **"This is what the LORD says: Do what is just and right. Rescue from the hand of the oppressor the one who has been robbed"** (Jeremiah 22:3).
  3. Will this strengthen the body of Christ and promote unity in the church? **"Carry each other's burdens, and in this way you will fulfill the law of Christ"** (Galatians 6:2).

- **Pray to God for guidance in the nuance.** Not everything will be cut-and-dried. Reject the idea that justice seeking in itself causes disunity (this claim can be a manipulative tactic). In fact, godly unity is brought on by truth and repentance. Certainly, things like physical or sexual abuse fall under biblical justice seeking, and those cases qualify as places to seek justice under multiple scriptural parameters. But things like spiritual abuse can as well. (Financial abuses can also qualify.) A trusted voice on the subject of spiritual abuse, Dr. Diane Langberg, author of *Redeeming Power: Understanding Authority and Abuse in the Church*, says: "Spiritual abuse involves using the sacred to harm or deceive the soul of another."[2] Under this definition, spiritual abuse can certainly qualify for seeking biblical justice.

- **Take the scriptural approach.** Remember that seeking justice is not seeking to take matters into your own hands by reckless vigilantism. God told us what to do in biblical justice seeking in Matthew 18:15–17:

> "If your brother sins against you, go tell him his fault, between you and him alone. If he listens to you, you have won your brother. But if he won't listen, take one or two others with you, so that by the testimony of two or three witnesses every fact may be established. If he doesn't pay attention to them, tell the church. If he doesn't pay attention even to the church, let him be like a Gentile and a tax collector to you." (csb)

God Knows Your Secret Struggles

[God] knows the secrets of every heart.

Psalm 44:21 NLT

I call the years from 2015 to 2017 my "worried-sick years," because those were the years my mother was a caretaker for my father, whose health was inexplicably declining. We knew something was wrong with him, but none of the diagnoses made sense for the severity of his mobility digression. I also knew, cognitively, that I was not his fixer—that worrying myself sick wouldn't do him or my mother any good. But sometimes we allow worry to boss us, and before we know it, it has infected our own bodies and minds. Worry had bossed me into thinking I had to manage the gravity of my parents' situation, and, as a result, pulled me into a sickness of its own: with isolation, lack of exercise, and low-grade anxiety, to name a few symptoms.

My parents lived a mostly private struggle of my dad's unexplained physical illness and my mother's dutiful insistence to care for him to the detriment of her own health. It was understandable in many ways—they had little money, few resources, and a historically take-charge man in the equation who didn't want random people taking care of him in a now-vulnerable state. There were no concrete answers about his condition, and the subconscious ingraining in that generation to not ask for help made matters worse. And so, my parents' struggle continued from months into several years.

Not having enough money to pay their bills, Mom taught art to kids in her home for some minor income, after getting Dad safely situated in front of the TV for a few hours at a time. Between that and social security, it kept them in their home.

But Dad's heart needed medicine, and these types of health problems don't come cheap. Purchasing thirty-day supplies of the medication was out of the financial question. So every day, mom would make a trip to the local CVS Pharmacy and purchase just two of his prescription pills at a time for him to keep living. The next day she would go again. And the next day, on repeat.

For two years, Dad's heart lived off mom's daily trips to CVS. Two pills, every day for two years. Just enough to get by.

And for two years, Mom's heart carried the heaviness.

No one on the outside knew about the two-pill-a-day ritual except for the pharmacist and God. Our money trail often tells the truest tale of our hidden struggles.

The mostly homeschool moms who brought their bouncy, eager kids for their weekly art lessons with my mother wouldn't have known—they were always greeted by the smiling, happy art teacher wearing an apron covered in dried paint. It wasn't a lie.

Momma *was* happy because her joy has never been about her circumstances. It's one of the things she has taught me: there can be moments of happiness and pleasure even with the companion of hardship. This confuses people when they refuse to honor the both-and of life. Life is hard and it is also good. They mostly live together.

> Our money trail often tells the truest tale of our hidden struggles.

No, the joy Mom had was specific. It was the core belief that despite the struggle, God is not unaware, and thus actively involved in the resolution of that struggle. That life was worthy to continue, even often in the dark. She had gotten used to the dark, quite frankly. Times were difficult for years. She had lived enough to know that God's ways were not going to be on her timetable or within her understanding. But she also knew trusting Him helped her endure, gain strength where she did not have it, and continue to be hopeful for the future. So that smile for her art students was, indeed, real.

> There can be moments of happiness and pleasure even with the companion of hardship.

We don't have to fake optimism when we believe in God's omniscience.

In these places of hidden difficulty, "*God knows*" becomes a quiet space of breath holding and prayers, where we trust for things like breakthrough, sustaining, and, if we dare, *hope*. We need God differently in these moments than when we want justice or to move past our past. Those things certainly prove equally in need of His omniscience. But urgency, rawness, and survival mark this particular space.

Sometimes our lives even depend upon it. Family members

with a drug-addicted loved one only really have the hope that God knows their pain over it, that He knows their loved one's enormous struggle, even, often, that He actually knows where their loved one is, since they haven't heard from them in months. My friend Jessica hasn't seen her meth-addicted daughter in a year. Summer came and went, without a word . . . then fall . . . and eventually, winter. Her Christmas presents remain unwrapped, waiting for her, if she ever comes to claim them. Spring brought flowers but no contact, and now it's summer, again, and still nothing. The hope they cling to is that God knows where their daughter is, and He is caring for her in their absence. Many parents cling to this.

The idea of struggle meets us in different places. Some of us have skeletons that have been so carefully kept sleeping we are terrified to do anything to awaken them. The thought that a secret we hold could be outed brings mixed feelings. On one hand, most of us want to break up with whatever is hurting us, but on the other, we want to be left alone with what has become familiar to us. Familiarity is the kryptonite of growth and often health and healing. It's an epidemic in safe Christianity. A companion in most unchanged lives.

What we know often makes us feel safe and comforted, and that is not automatically bad. There is real benefit to a relationship that makes us feel known, wanted, valued, heard, seen, and loved, no matter what—all of which play into feeling safe. But those desires and the ultimate desire to feel safe is met through God. Only God can bring us lasting comfort. Trying to meet those needs through a secret habit is

> Familiarity is the kryptonite of growth and often health and healing.

not only futile, but it is creating another entanglement that can take our reliance off Christ. More than one of us has fallen in love with something that we know good and well is bad for us, but we can't seem to let it go.

And then some of us struggle with secrets that aren't about things we have done but things that have happened to us that we desperately do not want. My friend's daughter has an unexplained illness that they've kept mostly quiet, but it keeps the whole family in daily confusion and pain. They are desperate for change. The secret struggle of this group of us is not being comforted by a habit; it is craving any type of comfort or relief. Making sense out of seeming nonsense or worse, cruelty. Wanting to understand how God could have insight into their daily difficulties and not intervene.

I don't know where you are with your secret struggle, what it is, or how it's affecting you. But what I do know is that when you find yourself furiously trying to hide or ferociously trying to fix or defend it, it is time to bring it to light.

God's omniscience allows Him a unique vantage point. He is aware of how deep in you are, how desperate, how much it will require His intervention to dig out—even more than you. So no, you are not alone in it. Someone already knows.

God wants to be our solution, in every way, no matter what our struggle winds up being.

Privacy Versus Secrecy

When we don't want to call something what it really is, we often call it something else.

God wants to be our
solution, in every
way, no matter what
our struggle winds
up being.

wants to be our

olution, in every

no matter what

r struggle winds

Like privacy.

Don't want someone to know about what you are doing? Close the door and claim it as private. *This is a private matter,* we say, and no one questions it. The word *private* often stops a conversation—it's one of the last universally accepted fences that gets you less pushback when you put it up.

Of course, we are absolutely entitled to personal privacy. No one should barge in on us in the bathroom. No one should be able to read a private text we send to our best friend. No one should be allowed access to our bank statements for the sake of being nosy about private finances. But that's not what the issue we are really dealing with is always about.

> **privacy** is about things that are personal that are important to keep fenced off from other people, for the good of our souls and/or the good of others.

We often call secrecy *privacy* when we don't want to get real about the struggles we are facing. We do this so we can buy more time with a habit we love and long to keep, keep up the facade to maintain a posture of perfection, keep trying to manage something out of personal pride, or even when we may not recognize the difference between secrecy and privacy.

They are, in fact, different. Like many things, the difference comes in the *motivation.* They are both things we keep to ourselves, but secrets generally benefit us, even when the "secret" is being kept on someone else's behalf. We still benefit by being the noble secret keeper, resulting in approval, feeding the need to people please—even those times it is a detrimental secret to someone's life or soul.

Private matters may be kept from being exposed, as well, but it is usually with the motivation of mutual respect, not merely self-interest. Sometimes we can convince ourselves that secrecy is what is best for everyone.

"If something comes out, it will only hurt them."

"If they don't know, it's for the best."

When we boil it down, it is most often what is best for *us*. Privacy is almost always a matter of respect—for the other person involved, and yes, for us too. God gave us a mind that houses private thoughts instead of giving us a mind that allows everyone to read our thoughts, hear them, see them. I've often thanked Him for the gift in that. But even with the respect that we intend with privacy, we have to be aware of how habits of hiding can develop.

> **secrecy** is about things we keep hidden from other people because we don't want to face accountability, behavior change, and/or repentance, or get needed help—to the detriment of our souls and many times to the detriment of others.

Sometimes, when we've been operating in secrecy for a long time and calling it privacy, it's hard to separate the two, even in our minds. Sometimes privacy can slip into secrecy, even when we don't intend it. It's why we have to keep a close eye on what we keep to ourselves.

My mother and father were private about many of their struggles when my father was still alive and in those difficult last years of his life. It was a habit long formed from years of being a "private" family in ministry. Most of that privacy with dad's health, mom's caretaking, and their finances was right and respectful. But the craving for privacy in my dad's pastoral years was what also got him in trouble. It wasn't as innocent as any of us wanted it to be. That's what privacy can become if we do not stay awake to it. This privacy-turned-secrecy cycle continued into my parents' eventual health and financial difficulties. The stakes were lower, but the emotional aspect was still costly. There were times we, as their family, wanted to help them but we often didn't know the moments they needed more help or to what degree they needed it. They wouldn't tell us because they didn't want to burden us. This resulted in frustration and sadness on our part, and eventually, with my mom, looking back, a measure of personal lament.

Sometimes it's hard to let people love you when you think you're loving them harder by refusing their help. But this isn't a love contest. In the end, when we don't let people into our needs, it just winds up hurting everyone. When we keep our struggles apart from people's prayers, we deny our own strength and healing. It is also contrary to what God intends. "Carry each other's burdens, and in this way you will fulfill the law of Christ" is not unclear (Galatians 6:2). We share our pain with each other *so that we honor Christ*. Like all things, even the privacy we get to enjoy is supported by the bigger mission of a life lived in fellowship with God and other believers.

We might think it's only our problem and keeping something private is our way of not burdening someone else, but that is often Satan's way of keeping us isolated without the help of community. Most of our secrecy is misguided self-sufficiency, when help is something God designed community and the church to provide in physical form so we would not suffer or

> Sometimes it's hard to let people love you when you think you're loving them harder by refusing their help. But this isn't a love contest.

recover alone. This is why we need Him and His infinite knowledge of the big picture so desperately—His instruction for us is a *process* that is for the good of our soul, while we try to quickly *make things good*. We often can't get better without someone beside us. Secrecy prevents us from accountability, behavior change, repentance, community, and getting well. Privacy generally won't do that, because while privacy doesn't expose things to the masses, it does let some close people in.

Is it privacy or secrecy that keeps you from getting help for your secret struggle?

Is it privacy or secrecy that keeps you from being honest about the difficulties you're having at home?

Is it privacy or secrecy that is preventing you from letting someone in who can provide support for a battle you are trying to face alone?

Is it a mix of privacy and secrecy and the lines have become blurred?

A quick way to assess secrecy versus privacy is to look at things you are spending a considerable amount of time trying to keep hidden. Hiding is not just an act of burying something; it can also be an act of not being forthcoming about it. Some of the ways this will make appearances: denial, deferring, blatant lying, strategy to keep it to yourself at all costs, avoidance of community or conversation. All this hiding leads to guilt or shame, which often leads to more hiding.

Trauma-informed therapist and author K. J. Ramsey frames shame like this: "Shame wants us to live divided, dishonest, disembodied lives . . . to let our lips say we believe God is good while our hearts stay discouraged in the dark."[1] The reason Satan wants you to keep things secret is because of the effect it will have on your soul. Even the chronic shame will become a burdening secret. This is another reason it is important to let people into our lives and struggles.

> Hiding is not just an act of burying something; it can also be an act of not being forthcoming about it.

Three simple ways to detect shame that has come from secrecy:

1. You avoid people you are keeping something from or to dodge a probing conversation.
2. You feel distant from God.
3. You feel negatively toward yourself for something you are doing that other people don't know about.

God doesn't want us to keep secrets because He doesn't want this kind of shame-filled life for us. He doesn't want us feeling negatively about ourselves, not enjoying relationship with people. Most of all, He doesn't want us distancing ourselves from Him.

Where do you need to let people into your struggle to help you? Where might God want to use your pain to help others even if your first instinct is to keep it completely to yourself? There is great redemptive power in reciprocal ministry through the sharing of burdens. Are you willing to let God use you to see someone else have a breakthrough in places that once broke you down? When you let God lead your story, that can be the result.

God isn't interested in a gotcha moment. He wants to help you have the courage to bring this out of a place of secrecy into the light for your good and His glory.

From the Inside Out

I've spent the past fifteen years studying Psalm 51.

If Psalms is the soundtrack for the many emotions of King David, Psalm 51 is, perhaps, its cover song. It is the guttural response of a man's contrite heart after being visited by a good prophet named Nathan, who confronted him for his sin with Bathsheba and subsequent plot to murder her husband. The whole situation was messy and horribly wrong. When you stop and think about the details for a minute, it involves sins that many of us would find unforgivable.

The story *is* one of forgiveness, though. David confessed and repented, and God forgave him, though not without consequence. God always knew about the sin. David might have thought he was keeping secrets, but there is nowhere to achieve true hiddenness from the omniscience of God.

A most famous verse, Psalm 51:10, is for many a personal favorite. "God, create a clean heart for me and renew a steadfast spirit within me" (csb). David knew that God and only God could give him a fresh start. The clean slate wasn't possible by mentally turning the page. Lasting renewal wasn't possible with a weekend retreat. Those things are great, but they aren't permanent solutions. The sins are too big, the struggles too consuming, the problems too vast.

If only a secret could be outed with no further complication.

There is nowhere

to achieve true

hiddenness from the

omniscience of God.

There is nowher

to achieve true

hiddenness fron

omniscience of

If only consequences wouldn't come with pain.

If only we could bypass the process of God to a quicker healing.

If only transformations were as easy as promises in a social media ad.

But David knew. None of his mess could be sorted out without God. He was the One with His eye on the problem the whole time because, as always, He was the One to provide the solution. It seems even in David's lust for pleasure and power, he was looking for God all along, which is our same misstep. As A. W. Tozer once said: "At the far-in hidden center of man's being is a bush fitted to be the dwelling place of the Triune God."[2]

No one else will ever fit in the spot in our heart intended for God.

In Psalm 51:6, David was expressing something we hunger for: that God might make us honest, from the inside out. "You delight in truth in the inward being, and you teach me wisdom in the secret heart" (ESV).

God wants us to have truth equal to breath. That we might keep no secrets from Him or anyone. He wanted David—all of David. Not a part. He wanted his integrity. His secret life. He even wanted the first *thought* of a secret life David was tempted to live. He longs for us to give him thoughts to crush, so they do not begin to tighten their grip on us and eventually lead us down roads like David took. Thoughts start us down those roads.

Psalm 44:21 says, "He knows the secrets of the heart," and since that is true, His omniscience dives into the innermost parts of our integrity. In case we have started to believe the lie of culture that the little things aren't important, that what we let into our hearts isn't all that important, let's not forget Psalm 44:21.

And if that feels intrusive, please also do not forget that God created that heart. He alone keeps it beating. He is the One to tend to it when it hurts or breaks. So consider the heart His specialty and, likewise, His business.

And just like with David, He is the One to create a newness within it, even as we confess to Him that which He already knows.

> **secret struggle**: something we keep hidden from other people that is consuming, dictating, or altering to our life in some detrimental way.

Your Secret Struggle

The interesting thing about our secret struggles is that when we picture them, we often picture them as selfish and dark. A struggle may get there, but often it starts with tenderness, feelings of helplessness over people or circumstances we can't fix or love enough to help. There are three important insights to remember as you think of your secret struggle.

Just because something is packaged prettier doesn't mean it's not causing us pain or keeping us from intimacy with God.

You might not be addicted to porn, but you could be equally committed to your perfectionism. Your desire to do things perfectly all the time may well have robbed just as much out of your life as something that on the surface feels much more sinister. Maybe it's that you love to shop, and it feels harmless, but that "harmless" habit has you hiding purchases from your husband.

I've seen the funny memes about this too. I've laughed at them. But is having to skirt around our actions really funny? Is it really harmless when things like this lead to debt that people struggle to get out of and relationships that get comfortable with not telling our spouse the full truth? I've gotten emails about wives struggling over secret credit cards. It happens a lot. Most important, does God know about the thing keeping you from living fully free, as He intended, and if He does, does it matter to Him what that thing looks like?

Satan is willing to take whatever moments he can get with you out of the game of serving God.

The truth is, slipping into things is much more common than jumping into them headfirst. This is because Satan likes stealth operations, so we don't immediately recognize his work. Entrapment requires the element of surprise.

Stay aware. Just because your struggle isn't heinous-looking and snarly or have you drug addicted and stealing out of your grandmother's purse, it does not mean it cannot entrap you or take valuable years off of your life. Satan is willing to take whatever moments he can get with you out of the game of serving God.

Getting into a struggle is one thing, but staying engaged in a struggle is another.

Don't let the surface good-naturedness of your secret struggle make you believe it's okay to keep hiding it from everyone who could help. And don't let the gravity of a deep, dark, difficult one make you feel it is too big or too out of control for God's intervention. You are responsible for the way you *engage* in a secret struggle by first allowing it *into* your life and then letting it *linger*. A lot of us are willing to own one but not both of these parts, but in the acknowledgment of them as a combination we are able to get the most thorough healing.

What allowed the struggle to be possible in the first place?

What has allowed it to continue?

Is there something there you can own?

Many times the reason we get into struggles isn't the same reason we stay in them. A struggle may feel familiar and even safe, as we already discussed, even though it hurts us. Maybe we don't know how to find our way out. Maybe we don't fully realize the depth of what we are in. We all have different reasons, but we aren't very different in how we approach them. We either settle for them, deny them, wrestle with them, or seek a way out. It is not that God is automatically having us endure a circumstance; it may be that we are unwilling to help ourselves do what it takes to get well. (I'll have a few ways to help at the end of the chapter!)

Our revelation about our struggle requires us to ask God for the insight only He has.

This is where God's omniscience comes so heavily into play in the context of our struggles. We simply cannot have the insight and wisdom to know ourselves this well, apart from Him. We cannot be unbiased to our own situation. We desperately need God to course correct our lives, like David did.

> **sin**: human activity that is contrary to God's will.

It would be normal to think, *It's hard for me to tell if a struggle I have has progressed when I am living through it.* That's fair. Sometimes, though, we lie to ourselves about this when we know the truth in our hearts. Frequency is a big indicator of progression. Unwillingness to let something go. Feeling like we need to exercise a behavior more and more or in order to feel peaceful, settled, or happy. Plotting ways to keep something that we can't bear the thought of parting with.

I know when I am in a place where something has a grip on me, I think about it often. I struggle to imagine my days without it. I don't want to be called out about it. I think in some ways, we could all say this about things like social media or our phones—the stealthy, silent killers of so many of our hearts and productive hours in the day.

The roots of secret progression in the Bible go back a long way—way back, to the night before Jesus' crucifixion. One commentary points out, "Consider, even, Jesus' 'secret' trial—The trial is full of anomalies: held at night, on the eve of a holy day, minimal attendance of members of the council, irregular location, without proper conditions pertaining to a capital case, no witnesses for the accused, and so forth."[3]

This commentary of Matthew 14–28 suggests such progression: what started out in secret eventually made its way to the open. Jesus had too much public appeal for the powers that be to have gotten away with the initial trial, so it all had to start out in a private setting—one might argue, *secret*, perhaps—so that the plan to kill Jesus would be carried out. Even something as powerful as the trial of Jesus started out as a covert operation.

With sin, this can sometimes be difficult to determine, though as the Spirit of God lives inside us, we should have that sense of conviction. This is where God's all-knowing is such a gift to us. When we do not have the wisdom to know if our struggle is a sin, He encourages us to ask Him who does. "If any of you *lacks wisdom*, you should ask God, who gives generously to all without finding fault, and it will be given to you" (James 1:5, emphasis added). Too often we underutilize this gift because we do not pursue the mind of Christ. A God with unlimited knowledge who would let us know where we are going wrong? One who would help us course correct without being judgmental? This is a God who can be trusted with our secret struggle.

Calling out the sin in your own life is good work, even when it's hard. We can't heal from things we don't name.

Like our daily lives, the circumstances of our struggles are all different. You might be the person who keeps a secret not because of some sin in your life or even a bad decision—but because your life is tied to someone who has deep needs. Don't let good reasons to do something or your desire to keep it together or not be a bother to someone allow you to slip into a life of secrecy.

> Calling out the sin in your own life is good work, even when it's hard. We can't heal from things we don't name.

You might have issues because someone you love has issues, and that has become your issue now too.

You might have chosen something that now has a grip on you, and you wish you could pull away from it, but you don't see a way out. You might not have meant to be where you are now—but regardless, you are there, and you need God to help you.

It is good to seek help. It is right. It is godly. It is not weak to go see a counselor or take medicine, for your body or your brain. It is strong. Sometimes we get too far into something to be able to see where the exits are. Let someone love you with a hand to lead you to the exit. God positions people all the time to do His work here on earth, so please don't push them away.

I have come to believe that sometimes even when people think they know us, they don't. And what we are willing to show people about us isn't always the true picture. God is really the only One who ever truly knows us . . . and all of it . . . and everything.

Because God knows my secret struggle, I don't have to live in fear of it being revealed.

Reveal: 3 Steps to Move Forward

1. Make a simple chart on a piece of paper. In the first column, write down the name of your secret struggle(s). In the second, write down at least one way it plays out in your life. In the third, write down a P for privacy or S for secrecy to show how you have been defining it. In the fourth, write a P or S for what it really is. Then write one to two sentences about what all of it is telling you.

2. Write down Psalm 51:6 and 10. Put these verses somewhere you can see them often. Memorize them over the next month, if possible. How do they encourage you to not be afraid to reveal your struggle to God, to a counselor, to a trusted friend or loved one?

3. Practice greater disclosure in your life by sharing with someone one thing that bothered you that day, one thing that excited you, and one thing you were working on. Do this at least three times per week.

God Knows Your Limits

"You are dust, and you will return to dust."

Genesis 3:19 CSB

The year 2009 ended my short-lived running career.

I call it a career, loosely, since it barely got off the ground. On a whim, while sitting on the couch one afternoon in air conditioning (where many great ideas are born), I decided to up the ante on my fitness and attempt a half-marathon—something I had never done before. I recruited my former-marathon-runner husband to train me, against both of our better judgments, knowing my penchant toward stubbornness and disdain toward this particular sport. Both of us were skeptical but hoped my determination would carry me to the finish line of this goal.

I'll spare you the specifics of what turned out to be a fast and furious three weeks ending in me throwing my running shoes to the back of my closet, not to be seen again until we moved out of the house ten years later—the important part is, I quit. It wasn't the training. It wasn't the coach. It wasn't the ability. It wasn't even that it was hard. It was that I felt limited. My mind told me I was limited. And so I was.

I am well aware of my privileged body that *gets* to decide to quit if it doesn't want to run. That is not the case for all of us. We are not limited in one accord. And yet, let us not be too quick to assume limits center on the physical. In her book *My Body Is Not a Prayer Request*, disabled scholar and lecturer Dr. Amy Kenny assures us of this: "To assume that my disability needs to be erased in order for me to live an abundant life is disturbing not only because of what it says about me but also because of what it reveals about people's notions about God. . . . My disabled body is a temple for the Holy Spirit."[1]

When God was speaking to Adam in Genesis 3 and said, "You are dust, and you will return to dust," He was referencing a human's greatest and yet most baseline limitation: that of *life* (Genesis 3:19 CSB). This is universal. His words to Adam simply mean that when God's breath (again, *rûaḥ*) leaves our body in death, our remains go back to where they originated—dust. ("The LORD God formed the man out of the dust from the ground and breathed the breath of life into his nostrils, and the man became a living being" [Genesis 2:7 CSB].) The reminder ties us, once again, to the omniscience of God in our appointed time of life on earth— which is limited and unmistakably purposeful. This understanding is a humbling one and makes us dependent upon Christ, in whom we "live and move and have our being" (Acts 17:28 CSB).

The great irony is that while our lives themselves are limited, there is no limit to what God can do with us in our lives.

The great irony is that
while our lives themselves
are limited, there is no
limit to what God can do
with us in our lives.

The great irony

while our lives t

are limited, ther

limit to what Go

How We Become Limited

Life's limitations are a result of one of these four things:

1. how other people limit us;
2. how we limit ourselves;
3. how we are limited by circumstances; or
4. a combination of all or some of these.

At least some of our unrealized potential stems from not being willing to do the work of understanding where our limitations came from. We haven't wanted to be honest, because it's been ingrained in us to cover for something we know deep in our bones was an overt bias—or someone hasn't listened or honored our story when we've tried, and we've settled for that. We have believed lies about our limitations or allowed what other people have said about them to skew our view about ourselves. Talking about this isn't in any way about blame or living in regret (both of which will continue to limit us)—it is about discovery and progress.

First, let's look at how we have been limited *by other people*.

How People Limit Us

People aren't to blame for what we do or don't do with our lives, but they can absolutely play a role as an influence. I fought for the personal faith I have, but having the mother I do made that journey easier. I watched a woman who modeled faithfulness and tenacity, and watching her planted deep roots. Not all things in my life have come with this privilege. I've felt, at times, held back by the opinions and actions of others. We all face rejection in life, and all rejection is not the same. Sometimes people not only influence the way we move through life, but they play a direct role in whether we do or do not move forward. In these situations, though it may seem like we are a victim to the decisions of others, God's omniscience has not changed. God is bigger than the limitation someone else wants to put on you. (Even if you are limited by it for a while.)

Unbiased Rejection

Unbiased rejection is the kind where people do not choose us based on criteria that are reasonable, without bias or malice. We may not like the criteria, but they are not unfair. We do not get the job because someone is more qualified or there is simply only one slot available and there has to be a toss-up choice. We do not get invited to a wedding because of limited seating and priority is given to closer family and friends. We invite friends over to our house for dinner and they don't come because someone in the house has been sick and they are concerned about spreading germs. These things sometimes still hurt, even though they aren't meant to be hurtful.

All of us have experienced them. They can limit us in our work if we don't get the job, even if the person who passed over us would not wish for us to be held back. This is simply a part of life. Inevitably, all of us will at times be in places like this, and in this unbiased rejection we may not feel seen or valued. These are natural feelings, and sometimes they are feelings caused by our own insecurities (we will talk about that more in a minute). But remember: the spiritual walk is a life of our constant sanctification. So even when we find ourselves awkwardly in a room that doesn't fully recognize our gifts and abilities, God can still use that to grow important places inside us.

Biased Rejection

Biased rejection is blatant and done with the purpose to exclude by personal, unjust reasoning. This is not only different from the tone of unbiased rejection, but it should also be dealt with differently. The limits it results in for the rejected party are real, causing true injury. Sometimes it is being bypassed for a position or held back from an opportunity due to prejudice from a powerful higher up. It might even be a friend group that refuses involvement because of someone's biased input, or a general bias against a certain group because of age, race, weight, gender, disability, or another factor that limits what someone in one of those categories is able to participate in if they are deemed unworthy or unqualified.

While sanctification molds us, shapes us, re-forms us into the character and likeness of Christ—which does require flesh to diminish—it will never compromise a person's dignity. This distinction can help us as we discern people's rejections.

There are rejections that are inexcusable. *Racial bias*, for instance, is blatant mistreatment. As a child of God, you should never have to ask any person to attach value to you, nor should you allow for someone else to be devalued on your watch, excuse it, or sweep it under the rug. Refusing to see and address clear bias is one of the great travesties not only in the world but in the church, which is to be a moral compass but has instead at times turned a blind eye to the dehumanizing of people to serve a cowardly self-interest. As a result, people have been gravely wounded internally, lives have been lost, community has suffered, turmoil has reached greater heights, and what people can do with the gifts God has given them has been limited by the sin of others.

Gender bias is an experience I have personally faced at times, to which nearly every female I know can in some way relate. A conversation about this is in no way meant to diminish men (I am the mother of two great young men), as the male gender should not be devalued to talk honestly about a historically systemic issue. Women have dealt with "jokes," sexualization, and diminishing of our gifts, and this is unacceptable. As a result, we have often been held back by fear, insecurity, and even cruelty. We have been limited by assumptions that we could not do jobs God has gifted us to do—never given the chance, yes, many times by men in the positions to extend them. Most women I know are not interested in competing with men; we simply want to do great work without being asked to prove our capabilities, differently.

I'm sorry to say that the bias toward women happens in-house as well. We women have at times limited each other. This grieves me, particularly, because we know more than anyone the struggles of our gender to use our gifts in this world, and yet we still sometimes put up roadblocks to each other rather than helping support and elevate one another. This biased rejection that causes us to forgo working with someone, recommending them, supporting, or promoting their good work or talent is often more about jealousy than bias, but the ramifications are the same. In some ways, this is one of the least-talked-about things among women but one of our biggest

> Most women I know are not interested in competing with men; we simply want to do great work without being asked to prove our capabilities, differently.

realities—so many of us have been limited by the pettiness of other females, in work, relationships, and in our own emotional progress. So it's critical to call it out.

Age bias is real as well, and so is *weight bias*. I've faced both. You would think in the Christian world those things don't exist, but they do. Today, I'm sad to say that especially in some circles it's gotten important to be physically attractive for Jesus.

In these and other overt biases, there will still be a choice. No matter who has limited us, we get to decide where we go from here.

Biased rejections can sometimes confuse us—make us feel like perhaps we share in the culpability. But it's not true. A person who is determined to shrink another person will find a way to do so. No person has the power to create their own scale of value to other humans. Remember that when you get that weird feeling that you aren't welcome in a room.

> A person who is determined to shrink another person will find a way to do so.

Remember, too, that you can't change an unhealthy person. Their unwillingness to deal with their brokenness is never about you. But you *can* refuse to allow that brokenness to affect your life any longer. A biased person is broken somewhere inside. They don't understand the kingdom of God. Only Jesus can mend a heart of bias; don't waste your time trying to change the unchangeable. People who need spiritual intervention cannot be helped by less intensive measures. You aren't responsible to fix someone who doesn't see value in all people.

People's rejection can't stop what God has planned for you. People's rejection can't take away your gifting.

People's rejection doesn't hinder your ability to thrive or move forward.

People's rejection is never really about you.

This rejection is a temporary setback. Move on. Press on. Trust that God has in mind incredible things for you to do.

How We Limit Ourselves

Limiting ourselves can develop into an unintentional habit over time. Sometimes things have happened in our past that have been stifling (unbiased and biased rejections, for instance) and as a result we have picked up where a bad experience has left off and limited ourselves further. Other times, like with my running, something we feel limited by (in my case, not being a good runner) leads us to truly become limited by our own blocked mindset. We will talk about this progression in the next section when I bring this all together, but for now, know that most often the things we need to deal with internally lead to external limits, so pay attention to the ways the Holy Spirit is prompting work that needs to be done in your heart. Those things then lead to other things, which have a tangible limiting result.

1. **Spirit of entitlement → leads to jealousy → results in people distrusting us = limited opportunity.** This is something the Lord spoke to me about personally several years ago. I wouldn't have known that's what it was, though, because I was too caught up in my feelings of not being included. I had been bypassed for a few events I thought I should have been invited to speak in, as well as

Trust that God has

in mind incredible

things for you to do.

attend an important ministry event as a guest, since many of my friends would be there. These situations happened simultaneously, and I found myself dealing with rejection. The natural feelings of wanting to be included would have been fine had I handled them properly with God. Instead, they were negatively influenced by the resentment I had allowed to grow and fester. It started to come out in negativity and a critical spirit. I had become jealous of those included, when I didn't used to be. During my time with the Lord one day, as I was praying and asking Him to give me more opportunities to serve Him, He spoke to me about what was really holding me back: a spirit of entitlement. Because I felt *entitled* to speak or be invited, I was becoming angry and resentful when those invitations didn't come. That spirit of entitlement led to a spirit of jealousy toward other people, and it resulted in stifling me from becoming the kind of person others wanted to invite in. Instead, it created further distance with community. If you find yourself being limited, do some soul-searching to see if there is a root of entitlement that might be holding you back. Often, that is at the core of our jealousy and critical spirit toward others, which can then cause people to naturally lose trust in us and shy away. We aren't entitled to God using us. We are invited into the honor of it.

2. **Spirit of insecurity → leads to neediness → results in people being drawn to those with more confidence = limited opportunity.** The struggle with insecurity has taken many people down. It is such a limiting spirit that it can look like everything from holding back from using

our gifts, to becoming inappropriately transparent online or in relationships in the name of honesty, to constantly asking for feedback as a means to determine worth in our work. We've all known people like this, or maybe, at least for a time, been like this. It never brings us the opportunities we want for friendship, love, or support in any career venture, because people are drawn to true confidence, not confidence feigned to cover insecurity. If you find yourself being limited, do some soul-searching to see if a root of insecurity might be holding you back. Often, that is at the core of our neediness, and even times of our pulling back to self-protect, which can then cause people to pull away from us. God doesn't want us to be limited by a constant struggle to see our worth.

3. **Spirit of self-focus → leads to stagnancy or frenzy → leads to resentment toward others/exhaustion to keep up = limited opportunity.** This spirit is an interesting one because it plays on opposite ends of the extreme. Either we become self-focused and frozen, which leads to stagnancy and results in resentment toward others and broken relationship; or we become frenzied in our attempt to conquer every opportunity and it makes us exhausted from trying to keep up. We struggle when other people move ahead. We spend enormous amounts of time wondering why we can't get where they are. We live in our heads, and we have short bursts of progress, but those are quickly met with all the ways we are held back and have reached our limits. A woman I know comes to my mind even as I write this. She is lovely, capable, well-respected, and limited by her chronic overthinking about herself.

I know because we've had many duplicate conversations about the things she wants to do, and they all have the same tone of self-focus. She loves God, but she cannot get out of her own way to use her gifts to serve Him. It's always complicated. Always unsure. Always overanalytical. And she never starts.

If you find yourself limited, do some soul-searching to see if there is a root of self-focus that might be holding you back. Often, that is at the core of our exhaustion, stagnancy, and resentment toward other people. If you have spent more time thinking about your capabilities (on either end of the spectrum), it is no wonder you lack opportunities to serve God. There's no time for focusing on both.

At the beginning of this chapter we talked about how there are absolutely circumstances in our life—tangibles—that limit us. These can range from finances to physical health, a lack of resources, connections, and opportunities due to geographical location or other circumstances. Limits of family issues, lack of support, and emotional resources exist for many people. We don't all have the same level of limitation because we don't have the same level of privilege—dependent upon even the country in which we live.

Regardless of the how, these are the ways we become limited. And in that, every bias, every rejection that was not done with malice but still hurt, every way we limit our own selves or were born into a set of circumstances

> If you have spent more time thinking about your capabilities, it is no wonder you lack opportunities to serve God.

we could not prevent or overcome by their very nature, is seen and known by God. This matters, because even in every story in the Bible of someone with limits, there was opportunity for healing, if only the heart. I say *only*, but really, the heart healing is everything. There was always tenderness and understanding. Always love. There was always faithful community of the Father. These are the things we can take comfort in, even as we are limited ourselves.

The sanctification of limits is undeniably a reason for them. For if we had no capacity, we would know no empathy for those living outside the margins. The way to help heal from the wounds of being limited by exclusion is to become a wild includer of others. Providing for others what you never got removes so much of the sting of your own past hurt.

> The way to help heal from the wounds of being limited by exclusion is to become a wild includer of others.

And in our limits we learn, too, what we really believe about them. And what we really believe God can do even when we can't.

Don't Let These Four False Assumptions Limit You

1. "God's power supply in our lives ends with our limitation."

   A core misunderstanding about God's attribute of omnipotence. An awareness of *our* limits is an invitation to embrace the *never-ending limits* of God. Our limits do not define God's abilities or pigeonhole God's strength.

2. "God's plan for us is biased/skewed."

   A core misunderstanding about God's love: we assume favoritism. Importance and useability become determined by human measurement. But God's plan for us supersedes our limitations, is never abusive or involves spin, and is focused on the kingdom of God.

3. "Our limitations negate the need to do and be more."

   A core misunderstanding about our own life agency and free will. We misunderstand our role as followers of Jesus, even in the construct of our limitations. Our lives belong to Him, yet we still have the ultimate responsibility to give Him the whole of them. It is not our place to determine how viable that life is.

4. "Our limitations are always a liability."

A core misunderstanding of God's design for boundaries to be beautiful. We resist the limits that were intended for our best, one, so we would rely upon Him for strength; two, for our protection. Limits are not a liability; in the kingdom of God they are leverage—for our weakness to be used by Him.

Real Limits Versus Limits That Become Real

I've long been fascinated by Jesus' encounter with a man in John 5, and for good reason—because this story of the man healed by the pool of Bethesda is legendary. It has all the makings of a perfect Bible story—all-powerful Jesus who miraculously heals a man after a long thirty-eight years, who didn't even recognize the work of the true Healer when He was standing right in front of him. How very on-brand for a human to not see God when He is right under his nose. But that's not where it stops. There was deflection to make the source of power about something it wasn't (v. 7—his faith in the healing waters of the pool). There was determination to insist on doing the same thing every day for all those years, expecting different results (*I'm trying to get into the pool, but someone always gets in ahead of me*). It's all the same old story we could tell about us.

But what I always come back to in this passage is the reality of limits.

The disabled man was no doubt physically limited and thus hindered from getting into the waters he believed would heal him. But there are suggestions in the text that he was limited in ways far beyond the physical: *his skepticism*—that he could ever be healed. (His first two words after Jesus' question, "Do you want to get well?" in verse six weren't "Of course!" They were, essentially, "I can't.") Then there was *his deflection*, as mentioned above, to make it about the pool instead of the true Healer. Even *his silence*, continuously allowing himself to be bypassed to get into the pool without speaking up. They were all limits.

This story from John 5 is important because it is a story of *real limits* and *limits that became real*. *Real limits* are most often caused by others and by outside conditions or circumstances. *Limits that become real* are those that, by virtue of another situation, turn into them. Sometimes these are limits we make for ourselves that were started by someone or something else. This man had *real limits*—he was physically unable to get into the pool. And he experienced *limits that became real*—his belief system was influenced by his skepticism, deflection, and skewed thinking that caused him to continue to be overlooked and not even recognize the Healer when He was standing before him.

There is undeniably a pattern in the miracle narratives of limitation in Scripture that requires overcoming with belief. Most often, there is a partnership between humanity acting and God healing. The lame man would never see the fulfillment of his healing *if* he didn't take the first step, which would have seemed absurd to him since he had concluded that taking a step wasn't possible (v. 8). And yet, we also know that we are never actually able. This is the rub and equally the mystery of faith. We also know that there are times we can fully believe God and He does not choose to heal us physically. This is where disillusionment can enter, if you believe healing is in our hands. It is also why it's important not to ever assume or suggest a person's lack of faith from the outside—it is, in fact, damaging and presumptive to do so. My precious girlfriend who had stage-four cancer was told this, which led her to deny getting treatment for a time in fear of not believing God enough. What heinous detriment loud outside opinions can cause.

People may seek to put limits on us, whether it is because they define us merely in terms of our bodies or circumstances or pressure us with hyperspiritual false narratives that persuade us to accept open-ended bias and unfair treatment in the name of goodwill. It is our responsibility to know the truth from Scripture and disallow other people to continue to limit us, to the extent we can. While we cannot control other people, we can change the way we are willing to be a part of groups and places, friendships and communities, and refuse invitations that do not honor us as people made in the image of God.

Sometimes, because the line can be thin, it can prove confusing. So here is a practical, side-by-side list of things that are close but not the same to help give clarity.

1. There's a difference between humility and false humility. Diminishing your abilities isn't being humble.
2. There's a difference between being proud of yourself and being prideful. Only one of these is toxic to your soul.
3. There's a difference between being kind and being nice. Kindness is a fruit of the spirit. Niceness is a people-pleasing tactic that typically turns out badly.
4. There's a difference between standing in your space and demanding someone to make space for you. Standing over demanding. It is so much more confident.
5. There's a difference between people tolerating you and people inviting you in. Only one of these is a good room to be in, for any length of time.

Pay attention to the way certain spaces make you feel. Don't go looking for those feelings of rejection or ostracism—in fact, go into places with an open heart, expecting the best. But as you are following the Holy Spirit, and having taken care of prior issues that could bias *you* to the situation, make sure you aren't

It is our responsibility
to know the truth
from Scripture and
disallow other people
to continue to limit us.

r responsibility

know the truth

n Scripture and

ow other people

trying to prove your worth, use your gifts, or stay in a space where people aren't valuing you for too long. Sometimes we do that when we don't know who we are in Christ.

For those times people have wanted to relegate us to what they assumed was our limitation, remember that our limitations are only a liability to humans. God knew we as humans needed them in our lives. First, so that we would rely upon Him for strength, as we talked about in the case of the man at the pool of Bethesda. We need to have a relationship of reliance upon God. Second, He gave us limits for our protection. This started in the garden, where He gave the singular limitation of one tree—the *knowledge tree*, remember—for the good of Adam and Eve. They didn't like that, just as we don't. But without limits, we will harm ourselves. This is where God's omniscience meets our limitation—He knows things about our life we do not, and He limits us to *protect* us. Paul said it best in 1 Corinthians: "'All things are lawful for me,' but not all things are helpful" (6:12 ESV). God truly does want to help us—this is why He has told us things we should and shouldn't do. We resist limits, but they are not a liability; they are a benefit. We just can't always see the benefit, so we struggle to believe and trust in it.

As well, in the spiritual realm, which is different from all others, limits are about *leverage*. Not our own leverage, because we don't belong to ourselves. But God's leverage of our limits. Second Corinthians 12:9 says, "He said to me, 'My grace is sufficient for you, for my power is made perfect in weakness.' Therefore I will boast all the more gladly about my weaknesses, so that Christ's power may rest on me." This is biblical leverage: that as we display our inabilities—limitations—Christ leverages them for the gospel. Divine combination.

And remember, there is another great equalizer, besides sheer humanity, in limitation. Even the limitations that go unseen are present in us all—the internal issues that hold us back, the past that continues to follow us, the silent health problem that isn't visible to the naked eye. Don't assume because you perceive perfection there is not hidden pain. Many people have smiled through struggle and laughed through loss. We are all creatively coping in some way.

> Don't assume because you perceive perfection there is not hidden pain.

Don't ever believe that your limits mean you cannot be more, do more, or thrive in the gifts God has given you. Knowing you have limits is not at odds with believing God can do more. The great lesson here is becoming accepting of our real and present limitations (in acknowledging we all have them as humans who are born of flesh and imperfection) and at the same time, understanding how many limitations have been made real by the way we have allowed them to become so.

What are your real limitations?

What are your limitations that have become real?

On this subject, I took a poll on my social media not long ago, and I wasn't shocked at the results. When I asked what their limits have been—either "mostly their own perceptions" or "truly limiting things," 74 percent said it was mostly perceptions and 26 percent said it was truly limiting things. This suggests that most of our limitations have become real because of the way they've affected our

> Don't ever believe that your limits mean you cannot be more, do more, or thrive in the gifts God has given you.

minds. They may have started out tangible or even continue to be tangible. But even true limitations aren't debilitating until they take up mental residence. That is when they go from obstacles to impasses, and we must overcome impasse situations that threaten to keep us stuck.

I took the social media poll a step further and asked for some examples of limitations, both ones that started out real and ones that have become real. The *real limitations* that made the list:

- Lack of resources—a lack of time or money
- Lack of opportunities—due to gender, age, size or race biases, family of origin/upbringing, experience, geographical location
- Limits of physical and mental illness/disabilities
- Limits of family issues/abuse/dysfunction/lack of support

These things can and often do hinder us. They are real and complicated. Not everyone will understand them or know exactly how they have affected our lives. We all come from different starting points in life. It's just not true that everyone has the same opportunities and should and will operate out of an identical place.

And because, like in much of life, we hold the tension of two truths, we face choice even in our very real limitations. The man at the pool of Bethesda had physical limitations that prevented him from walking into a pool for healing. But he needed healing of the mind and heart more than that. Those limitations were more binding.

John 5 is the story of both; and many times, we are the story of both. You may be truly limited, but that's not where it has to end for you. The question of "Would you like to get well?" like Jesus asked isn't just about that real limitation you so desperately want to not be a part of your story. It is about what you *believe* about that limitation, what you believe God knows about it, and what He wants to do with your life still.

> You may be truly limited, but that's not where it has to end for you.

When I asked my social media followers, again, to tell me what were their *limitations that had become real*, the list was even longer. Specifics about many things boiled down to these categories:

- Our skepticism—based on hard things that have happened in the past we struggle to move past, believe, or have a positive outlook on the future
- Our doubts—that we can be or are the right person for the job or that God can use us
- Our insecurities—that we can be enough, are seen or heard; becoming a bottomless pit of needing encouragement
- Our people pleasing—constantly striving for approval and being exhausted by it
- Our pride/rigidity—that it should be done our way and the way we see it is the only right way
- Our trust issues—struggling to believe anyone or anything
- Our comparison and jealousy—difficulty being happy for anyone else or constantly comparing ourselves to someone
- Our perfectionism—the need to have everything completely perfect and together before we can move forward in any way; our cruel expectations for even ourselves

- Our guilt and shame—replaying our past and the mistakes we've made
- Our fear—of failure, rejection, abandonment, lack, not knowing enough, disappointing God, that we won't be enough or have enough resources in the future
- Our shortsightedness—our impatience to make quick decisions, choosing the right-now thing instead of the thing we want and need most and is better for us in the long run
- Our desire for temporary comfort and relief—numbing tactics to defer healing that often hurt us more
- Our perceptions—the mental games we play that assume and keep us overthinking about people and things

What a list.

Is it clear to you too?

We are limiting ourselves much more than we are actually limited.

Your limitations don't scare God, bother God, hinder God, or surprise God. Therefore, they should do none of those things for you. He wants you to break free from the things that encumber you, yes. But He can work around your less-than-perfect scenarios. He doesn't need you to become flawless. He doesn't need you to be of a certain age, born into privilege with the right last name, or have the genetics that make you socially the right packaging. What truly limits us is the obstacle of the optical. Your life will change when you begin to see limitations as opportunities for God to show forth His greatness.

What truly limits us is the obstacle of the optical.

Unlimited God

When we live in some form of actual reality of "I can't" like the man at the pool of Bethesda, when we have limited ourselves, when others have limited us, we need to believe God's power is not compromised by our obstacles.

Most of us know this. Many of us believe it is true. We are hopeful, perhaps fearful, and sometimes skeptical, though, when real life rubs up against our theology. Skepticism that leads to a search for the truth can make us a believer, but left unchecked, it can be our biggest limiter. When we maintain a critical eye on what we believe God can do, we never truly exercise trust in Him. It is a way for us to self-protect in case we decide to play small.

The problem with that is, we never get to experience much. God doesn't want us to live like that. He wants to thrill us with an expanded version of our life. He wants us to feel confident that He is fully God, able and working, in our limits too.

I know it is often difficult to believe, or believe again, in the midst of our limits. Our habits and sins that limit us require soul work. When we've been limited by someone else, breaking out of that takes a mental, emotional, and spiritual commitment and process. We may question, at, times, if it's worth it. But as Helen Keller, disability-rights advocate, political activist, and lecturer who knew much about challenging limitations, once said: "The hilltop hour would not be half so wonderful if there were no dark valleys to traverse."[2]

It truly is more incredible to watch Jesus do in and through us things that without Him are impossible.

Even in our trust of Him, we must trust that He knows the best result. Sometimes our prayers will be answered. Sometimes what needs to change is for us to do the work of belief and faith so our hearts become different. Sometimes we need a miracle to loosen our limits, and He brings us one. Sometimes we learn to rest in what we cannot change. But always, there are greater places to go with God.

Author Madeleine L'Engle wrote in her book *Walking on Water*: "We have to be braver than we think we can be, because God is constantly calling us to be more than we are."[3] Yes, God is calling you to more. God is calling all of us to more.

Part of that calling to more is to begin to take our eyes off ourselves in this whole issue of limitations. It can become easy to think our circumstances are about us, and certainly there *is* importance in our steps to growth and progress. But ultimately, our limits are to show the glory of God. The very thing we may feel stifled by, God may want to use to set other people free. This is a high calling—a calling to more.

John 9 beautifully illustrates this higher calling in the healing of a blind man. His life—a life born with visual limitation—was created to bring honor and glory to God. And *it did*.

> As he went along, he saw a man blind from birth. His disciples asked him, "Rabbi, who sinned, this man or his parents, that he was born blind?"
>
> "Neither this man nor his parents sinned," said Jesus, "but this happened so that the works of God might be displayed in him. As long as it is day, we must do the works of him who sent me. Night is coming when no one can work. While I am in the world, I am the light of the world."
>
> After saying this, he spit on the ground, made some mud with the saliva, and put it on the man's eyes. "Go," he told

him, "wash in the Pool of Siloam" (this word means "Sent"). So the man went and washed and came home seeing.

His neighbors and those who had formerly seen him begging asked, "Isn't this the same man who used to sit and beg?" Some claimed that he was.

Others said, "No, he only looks like him."

But he himself insisted, "I am the man."

"How then were your eyes opened?" they asked.

He replied, "The man they call Jesus made some mud and put it on my eyes. He told me to go to Siloam and wash. So I went and washed, and then I could see."

"Where is this man?" they asked him. (John 9:1–12)

People are looking for miracles. They don't know it, but what they are really looking for is Jesus. There is no higher calling than for God to use your life to show people who He is.

Will you allow God to use your limits to bring Him glory?

Will you trust that He knows how to work despite your limitations?

Will you let Him expand your limits and take you to more?

You might not get the miracle that causes people to stand in awe.

But God will always change your heart.

Because God knows about my limits, I can rely on His limitlessness.

Rely: 3 Steps to Move Forward

1. Look back at the list of ways we become limited. Which apply to you? Pray and make an action plan to take a step toward breaking free from whatever it is that has been holding you back. Write it down and tell it to a trusted friend or family member for accountability.

2. Reread the story of the man at the pool in John 5 in the context of his limitations. Consider your own life. How can working on your limitations change how God uses your life?

3. Look back at the "practical notes" list of things that are similar but not the same. Which of these most applies to you? Write an "I will . . ." statement out of it and put it somewhere you can see it every day to help you remember what to pray about and to inspire you for more.

Practical Tips for Humble Soul-Care

1. Be able to say you are proud of yourself.

   Squashing our victories to make people feel more comfortable, less jealous, or to feign meekness isn't humility. The real thing isn't about diminishing personal wins.

2. Be willing to advocate for your gifts.

   When you feel stifled by bias or assumption, first make sure you've taken care of heart and soul issues; and if you have, check to see if you're in the "wrong room." Don't stay in a room in which you constantly feel you must fight to use your gifts or prove your worth.

3. Be sure to show up for yourself.

   Denying oneself spiritually isn't about allowing poor treatment from other humans. It's about deference to Christ. Dying to self doesn't require you to be devalued.

06

God Knows Your Past

As far as the east is from the west, so far has
He removed our wrongdoings from us.

Psalm 103:12 NASB

A few years ago, I was speaking in a city in which I spent
a lot of my younger years—the kind of place that holds the history where you cut your teeth on regrettable teenage decisions like hair dye, fast driving, and a snotty attitude that people with a very good memory never let you forget. A private introvert, a sometimes-outspoken preacher's kid, and an insecure girl who never quite recovered from being called fat by her very first crush, teenage Lisa was *complicated*. If I could wrap young Lisa up in my arms now, I would hold her tenderhearted self so tight and tell her that assertive women wouldn't be so misunderstood one day, that self-protecting with your fists up doesn't make for

very good relationship-building, and that Jesus is the only One who always needs to be strong. This is what she needed to hear, instead of words of scrutiny and judgment.

Though I'm grateful to speak wherever God sends me, every speaker knows it is a mixed bag to speak in a place you grew up. This is no exception. But my circumstances exacerbate it. My hometown is also the place my father had a very public ministry fall, lost his church, and our family was all over the local news. Memories are harder in this place. Speaking is heavier because it comes with baggage.

I am in the greenroom before the first night of the event, and it is mere minutes before I take the stage. I am prayed up, prepared, and feel ready, *until* . . . an offhanded comment by someone sitting in the room threatens to break me. We are talking about someone we both know from our past, and I am told that when she found out I was the one speaking, she declined the invitation to come to the event because she couldn't get past who she knew me to be in high school.

It's amazing how quickly a moment like this can cause that young version of ourselves to resurface, how quickly comments can be used as tools of discouragement, how people who don't let you forget the places you've worked hard with God to move past don't realize how damaging their skepticism and negativity really are.

I have lived away from this city for nearly thirty years. Been through rounds of counseling. Enjoyed a monogamous twenty-seven-year marriage, raised three wonderful kids, kept the same best friend since seminary, successfully house-trained a small dog, and managed to not kill three current houseplants. For most of my adult life, God has allowed me to serve in some incredible places in ministry, using my gifts. Most of all, He has changed me so much since my high school and college days, sometimes even to myself I am unrecognizable.

Yet at this moment, none of it feels like enough. I am not allowed to forget. My past missteps have disqualified me from standing before people and saying to them, "God loves you. You can change. You were made to be used for the glory of God," even though it's my actual testimony. Only perfect people get to do that. Only people who haven't made mistakes. I wish I knew people like that. Someone. Anyone. I know for sure: it is not me.

I'm guessing you have some type of "that is not me" story because of something in your past. Maybe it's made you think as a result, *That can never be me*, as far as what God can do through you because of things you've done. If someone else hasn't put that on you, you have put it on yourself. We are good at preaching our own inadequacies, self-diagnosing our own dead ends and ceilings. People are good at being historians, especially when the history involves someone else's shortcomings. But God knows about that past you cannot redo. You would if you could. You wish you could. But wishing is really just wasting—wasting time, wasting energy, wasting years of your life that could be used to glorify God with your gifts.

It would be one thing if God hadn't been aware of your past and chose you without that information. But His omniscience covers for every hidden sin, your most heinous secret, and your worst behavior, past and present. It's not like with other people, where they don't know everything— they only see your good

> We are good at preaching our own inadequacies, self-diagnosing our own dead ends and ceilings.

side and love you with missing information. We don't have to wonder what God *might* do if He knew even *that*. He does. And it hasn't changed anything.

At the same time, it is the reason we are ever-needy of Him. Because of what He knows about our private life, He says: "'My grace is sufficient for you, for my power is perfected in weakness'" (2 Corinthians 12:9 csb). Paul, who wrote this, *of all people*, had experienced the joy of coming into fellowship with a God who knew every sordid detail about what he had done and yet not only forgave him but chose to powerfully use his life moving forward—the same thing He wants to do with ours, no matter where we've been or what we've done.

Is It Over for You?

It's not over for anyone until God gives that word.

Literally, of course, in death, but also, in life. With the information in front of us, most of us would call curtains on someone long before their comeback, and often, it could be justified. By the looks of where we are headed or the mess of where we have been, there is no proof of turnaround. That is why the sovereignty of God is vital. Without it, we would be making judgment calls that were incorrect. We would be stopping people from years of their greatest usability in the kingdom of God. So what God knows about our past and how He is going to redeem it in the future is everything.

Paul is one of the more

> **What God knows about our past and how He is going to redeem it in the future is everything.**

famous turnaround stories in the Bible, but he is certainly not the only one. Jonah, who ran from God, became greatly used by Him to evangelize a wicked Nineveh. Rahab, a prostitute, became the reason two men and her entire families' lives were saved. Gideon, once fearful, became a warrior. David, immoral and murderous, became someone who followed after the heart of God.

Moses murdered a man too. Some might argue that he was justified, but ultimately life and death are in the hands of God.

> Years later, after Moses had grown up, he went out to his own people and observed their forced labor. He saw an Egyptian striking a Hebrew, one of his people. Looking all around and seeing no one, he struck the Egyptian dead and hid him in the sand. (Exodus 2:11–12 csb)

Could God still use someone like this? Moses was now a murderer. Scholars argue whether this murder was truly sin because of the circumstances, but we can agree that this part of his past surely affected him. It likely affected the way he went into the future and, even more specifically perhaps, the way he felt unqualified to lead. Memories of past hardships have derailed many people on the road to serve God. We know from Scripture that Moses struggled with leadership and even asked God to replace him with someone more qualified. Often, when we live in our past, it affects our confidence in tasks for the future. Moses was plagued by a lack of confidence in what he felt he was able to do.

> Moses replied to the LORD, "Please, Lord, I have never been eloquent—either in the past or recently or since you have been

speaking to your servant—because my mouth and my tongue are sluggish." The LORD said to him, "Who placed a mouth on humans? Who makes a person mute or deaf, seeing or blind? Is it not I, the LORD? Now go! I will help you speak and I will teach you what to say." Moses said, "Please, Lord, send someone else." (Exodus 4:10–13 CSB)

There's a deeper importance here when it comes to what God knows about your past and using you despite it. It's not that we just miss out when we stay stuck back there. It's that we can actually work *against* God in His plans for us. God is more powerful than us. But He will not strong-arm us into compliance. Insisting on living in our shame and insecurity over our past is counterintuitive to a forward-thinking gospel. "'Forget the former things; do not dwell on the past. See, I am doing a new thing! Now it springs up; do you not perceive it?'" (Isaiah 43:18–19). It also causes much of our internal angst, because negative memories will fill our minds with negative thoughts if we don't refuse them.

People struggle with their own past, so there will always be someone who doesn't want to let you forget a time you messed up. Those who haven't fully come to peace with things like forgiveness or grace will be inclined to treat mistakes like ransoms. The fact that you were young and your best-reasoning days were ahead of you, you were sleep-deprived that day, you just heard the news you lost your job, or you had a raging migraine and shouldn't have answered that email at that moment won't be given consideration. Sometimes we give excuses for people when we should hold them to a standard, but far more often we render judgment on them while we excuse ourselves. Canceling people wouldn't be so popular if there weren't an eager market for it. There will always be people who will hit replay, always people who don't care to find out the backstory, always people who will make up their minds without asking the source. There will always be people who feed into your *own* insecurities about things you've done in the past, even when you've moved on from them.

When they do, you'll probably want to defend yourself.

But I want you to know when that happens, if you have made it right with God and you have made the things He has nudged you to make right with other people as best you can, you are okay. Someone else's issues have nothing to do with you. Even when they do, it is not your job to convince them you are a changed person. You may have heard the Bible verse in Romans 8:31: "If God is for us, who can be against us?" This is a verse in the same passage about life lived in the Spirit. Verse 1, equally notable and along the same lines of heavenly support but taking it even a step further, says, "Therefore, there is now no condemnation for those who are in Christ Jesus." Do not waste time on overapologies to people about things you and God have already resolved.

Time wasted on overapology for your life for the kingdom of God.

And there is this from Psalm 103:12: "As far as the east is from the west, so far has He removed our wrongdoings from us" (NASB).

> Do not waste time on overapologies to people about things you and God have already resolved.

East from the west—the eternal distance of measurement. There is not one thing from the past not covered by the expanse of forgiveness here.

At the same time, we are not without personal responsibility. If you feel like you are constantly having to try to prove your worth—over the past or in the present—consider how much time you are spending living in the opinions of others. While we cannot control how they view us, we *can* control how much *we think about how they view us*. And we can also control how we think about ourselves. As with everything, thoughts are only allowed to continue if we give them that access in our minds.

There's a great balance of humility, personal ownership, and the wisdom not to carry someone else's labels for us in a life of faith. It is being duly committed to the work of change while grateful for the good work that God has already done in us. Famed poet and author Maya Angelou writes so beautifully of this tension: "History, despite its wrenching pain, cannot be unlived, but if faced with courage, need not be lived again."[1] With Jesus, we never have to rewrite history. God is gracious to give us insights into how our past informs us and even more gracious to wipe away the shame of it. We don't have to pick between having work to do and being proud of the work we've done to get better. God wants us to recognize both, and in them, our desperate need for Him.

Maybe it's guilt and shame you carry from years of reckless living, and you have internal things you need to deal with. *Okay*. For your sake and the sake of all your relationships, go deal with that. But be willing to also evaluate your delay up to this point. Was it a need to deny pain? Pretend away a hard past? Preserve an image? If it was any of these things, it has undeniably cost you. Shame and guilt are soul killers. Caring so much about the way we present ourselves that we are willing to die inside to do it is a terrible payoff. If that is where you are, I am praying you'll be set free from it, because God knows *everything*. And He has not turned away. There is no one to be ashamed in front of when the Highest and Greatest knows it all about you.

Approval Versus Apology

Before we make any progress, we have to take people off the pedestal with God. Besides the fact it's idolatry (a sin), the disappointment and disillusionment it causes our souls when a human fails to provide for us what only God can is weighty. (And it's a leading reason why some people no longer believe in the church or spiritual leadership.) It changes the way we look for approval from them to give us second chances, appreciate our progress, and even know details about our past that only an omniscient God could possibly be privy to. It is not too much to ask people to support change in us. But they won't believe in us the same, love us the same, forgive us as readily or thoroughly. God will not hold grudges, but people will, and no matter what we do we will not be able to right a wrong. If you are exhausted from the realities of this, please consider that people have become too important in your process.

Once we've taken people off the pedestal, we can deal with the true issue at hand: how much of our past we should feel responsible to even revisit with them. In many cases, people will expect more from us in this regard than is necessary or reasonable. You do not owe people you have not wronged explanations about your past. However, here are three groups of people it is good to revisit your past with:

1. **People you have personally wronged whom you need to apologize to.** (We will talk more about this in a minute.) This is a cut-and-dried scriptural command.
2. **People you feel God leading you to discuss an issue of the past with, in order to achieve greater**

143

transparency, accountability, healing, community, and understanding. This is less direct in Scripture, but it is certainly implied and applies Holy Spirit wisdom and common sense.

3. **A counselor who can help you with past issues affecting you presently, in order to help you heal and move forward in your life.**

Beyond these categories of people, it will be a matter of deciding whether the conversation about your past would be fruitful for the kingdom of God. Rely on Him and not others to determine that. Treat your past with respect and consideration. God has done a great work to restore you from its hard places, and sharing it should be done with freedom and thoughtfulness, love and care. All our pasts should be viewed in the context of redemption and are ultimately about Christ, not us.

Many of us get caught in the trap of thinking we must revisit the past in order to make it right. This might even be a pure-hearted motive but still be offtrack. We have to understand the difference between (a) wanting to explain ourselves so we aren't misunderstood (an underlying issue of people pleasing), over-apologize for the past, and continue feeling bad about it, and (b) offering people an apology for things in our past that need to be made right. The former is for approval and is not a part of true apology. I call it "pitching ourselves to people," because that's exactly what it is like—a salesperson pitching a product to get people to buy it—except in this case, we are pitching the product of ourselves.

New and improved! You won't believe the difference!

Just give me a chance—I promise you won't be disappointed.

Read all my positive reviews! See how many other people love me?

I hope you'll buy in!

Before we know it, we have spent more time selling ourselves to people than living our actual lives. The point of all our stories isn't nearly as much about how we used to be—it's all about who God has changed us to be. Staying hungry for people to stamp *APPROVED!* on us keeps us stuck in a place we have already left behind. Living to prove to them we are now worthy of their time, attention, belief, and love keeps us focused on people who are equally in need of the same things. So it becomes a futile pursuit and endless cycle.

We have to stop pitching ourselves to bad listeners. To the right people, we won't have to pitch ourselves at all. People who invite you back into the past are often stuck there themselves and just want some company. No one can make you go back there. You have a choice, even if you once did not. It is wise to no longer allow people to pick your emotional and spiritual destinations. When you apply this, no one can pull you back into the past unless you give them that permission. Turn down all invitations to live in regret and overapology. Refuse to revisit confessed sin. Be grateful for, not ashamed of, healed sickness. Be humble about how God has changed you and unapologetic about how you've done the work to become a different person. Jesus changes everything *and* He expects us to change too.

The best way to show someone you are not the same person you were in the past is to live your life differently and let them notice the difference. Changed people can't hide a good transformation.

Apologies, though, are very different from the approval game

> Be humble about how God has changed you and unapologetic about how you've done the work to become a different person.

and are often what is needed when you've hurt other people in the messiness of your past. There's nothing more powerful than someone who owns their damage to other people and nothing more harmful than someone who denies it. It's too tender and personal to tell the details of the story here, but little would I know that on that same speaking-event trip in 2016, God would allow me to see someone else in my hometown to whom I would get the opportunity to offer a long-overdue apology. Unlike the woman who refused to come to the event, to whom I didn't owe an apology or even an explanation, to this woman, I did. When we were young I had not been the friend to her that I should have been. And God in His graciousness allowed me to see her after all that time and distance and apologize to her for all the ways that I might have affected her. It certainly had affected me. When we live with a bottled-up apology, we stifle our own healing.

Do you need to apologize to someone for something in the past? Don't wait another day. Many people regret withholding one—few regret making one. Wanting approval and pursuing apology isn't the same. When we pursue apology, we pursue peace with God. He sees and knows our humility. Even if someone shares in the responsibility of what we are apologizing about for the past.

And one more thing about this. Sometimes people will tell you how you've hurt them in the past, and it's important to really hear them, even if you don't remember it or it didn't impact you like it did them. Marks are made on the soul differently, so you can't compare yours to theirs. Hear people. Listen. Pray about what they've said and what they need now. Dismissal of someone's memory only adds another layer to their pain.

Do your part. Own your past. Make it right in the best way you can.

And then move forward.

> Do your part. Own your past. Make it right in the best way you can. And then move forward.

Boundaries

We can't talk about people and our pasts without talking about our need to do better with our relationships in the future. Many of our issues we have had to repent from, ask apologies for, and get healing over had to do with broken or unestablished boundaries, so it is worth spending a few minutes on it.

It's hard for a lot of us to set boundaries because we don't know how to separate love from access, acceptance from companionship. Many of our issues with relationships from the past have been about our lack of boundaries.

It's why we've gotten into bad relationships.

It's why we've burned out.

It's why we've ended up resenting people.

It's why we've compromised our morals.

It's why we've wound up quitting on our dreams, relationships, and serving God.

It's why we've collected more shame and regret, repeating past mistakes.

It's why we've lived with a closed heart instead of an open

one, because we give ourselves no better alternative to keeping negative and damaging people out.

Boundaries are often the best way to love people, including yourself. Arrogance (and ignorance) says we can help everyone with no parameters. That was not the role we were made for; it is a role that only God can fill. Maybe you believe that, but these are some of your thoughts:

I love the idea of boundaries, but I'm just not good at them.

Isn't rejecting people unkind and unspiritual?

Don't boundaries separate us from each other?

You might think these things if you don't understand how omniscience plays into the importance of boundaries—what God literally created in the garden to show us *in the beginning* the model for our best. He told His first created humans where they could and couldn't go within a place He created for them, and He gave them specifics about what they could and couldn't eat. Their need for boundaries was established out of His vast wisdom (a.k.a. God knew!) about what was best for them—not out of cruelty, aloofness, or punishment. When the boundary was broken, there were consequences, and we experience them to this day. The freedom from our past and the quality of our relationships in the future (even our relationship with ourselves) hinges on our own understanding of how fully known we are by God. Back to 1 John 3:20 again: "If our hearts condemn us, we know that God is greater than our hearts, and he knows everything." We honor the boundaries within His heart for us. It's all quite full circle.

Boundaries will help keep you from having to regret any

> **Boundaries are often the best way to love people, including yourself.**

more moments. They are such an important way to do relationships. Here are three practical boundary suggestions.

1. **Become so committed to your boundaries you only have to verbalize them 10 percent of the time to other people.** The other 90 percent of the time people can already tell what they are, or at least that you have them.

2. **Release the need to convert everyone to liking your boundaries.** You don't need people to agree with them in order to have them—in fact, most of the time, the people you most need to set boundaries with won't like them.

3. **Choose your life travelers wisely.** I'll use a figurative example here: think of the heart and your car as two different places of both access and capacity for people in your life travels. Having room in your heart—a God-given space with capacity to love and honor all people (a whole bunch you can "pile in"), and having room in your car—a much smaller space in which to take a limited number of passengers with you—are two very different things. See your most trusted people, the ones who encourage you and make you better, as your car travelers. You will love all people, but you will travel with far fewer. Be selective about those car travelers. Combative, demanding, degrading, or directionally opposed (to Jesus) people cannot ride in the car with you. They are dangerous distractions to where you are going in life.

Having boundaries is truly going to make all the difference in the world as you move forward. With people, for yourself, and in the way you begin to recognize them as a gift from God.

God Isn't Judging You

God knows everything about your past.

When you read those words, do you feel loved? Known? Judged?

We've come from many different places to arrive here in these pages. The way we view God is directly tied to many things—how He was presented to you from an early age, a church or denominational background, childhood and upbringing. God has been tarnished by our inept earthly relationships. Often, worse than that. So if your mind immediately goes to judgment when I say *God knows*, I fully understand it, but you have the wrong impression of God.

So let's talk about the right one.

We can be sold some junk theology along the way of life, and before we know it, we form complete narratives about God that aren't true. If God has been presented as a hard-nosed taskmaster, it will be hard to ever believe in rest—surely God wouldn't want us to stop producing. If He has been pitched to us as foreboding and critical, we will want to cower in our shame when we sin. There is a big difference between firmness and harshness, conviction and feeling diminished. I love the way *The Message* paraphrase makes such distinctions about God in Romans 2:4: "God is kind, but he's not soft. In kindness he takes us firmly by the hand and leads us into a radical life-change." I see it, don't you? It's somehow both with God. Kind, but not soft. Kindness that leads to something strong and radical.

God convicts us so we might return to communion with Him; the motive is love, never retaliation. Will He be firm about it? Likely. We need God to lead us well, and leadership involves course correction. But will He be harsh? No. It is not in God's nature to handle His creation with a cruel hand.

This is important to reconcile because to be completely set free from your past, you must value the truth that God knows all about it. Otherwise you will always try to hide a part of it from Him. You must, in fact, be grateful that He knows, so no hiding is necessary. When we do not waste time trying to conceal our past from God or live under the shame of it, He can do the proper work of healing it.

And His knowing it already is freeing because it means that while confession of sin is an important aspect of a healthy spiritual relationship, it is also not going to be a surprise to God. Putting it very simply, we won't be shocking God with any news about our past wrongdoings. This should come as some relief—to not have to explain our entire backstory. Back in the garden, where all our waywardness started, the gross misconception of Adam and Eve was that hiding would bring comfort, when in fact it was the very thing that brought sorrow. Not just for that moment but for generations. Attempts to avoid doing it God's way always affect more than just us. Anyone who has ever tried to hide anything from God knows that in its moot-ness there is also grief, because we scramble to keep something good from our own souls. And many times, *we achieve it.*

> To be completely set free from your past, you must value the truth that God knows all about it.

So God being omniscient as it relates to our past is such a gift. It creates a spirit of constant openness. There is nowhere to hide with God, and it is not necessary. We truly cannot say this with anyone else.

Judge: the holy characteristic of God as the ultimate Ruler and Decision-Maker of the world and our lives

judgmental: a human characteristic God in His nature cannot embody (excessively critical, fault-finding)

God is the great and ultimate Judge, ruling over the world and our lives, as is told to us all throughout the Bible. But he isn't judgmental, which is another important distinction. And, too, there is accountability with His position. This is how God works in our lives and works things for our good.

Repentance (us) + Forgiveness and Redemption (Him) = a most thorough life change. It's an incredible process.

God knows you. He loves you. He chose you. He sees you. He is tender to your struggle. He fights for you. And He is coming for you.

Please don't get the wrong idea when you hear that He knows all about your past. If He didn't know everything, when you read about Him loving you and promising to never leave you, you would suspect that to be conditional. It would be like many of the rest of the humans we know, who at some point reach their limit and do not stick around. As it stands now, you know it is a solid promise that will not change, no matter what. God knowing about your past is your guarantee that there is nothing you can do in your future that will make Him quit you, because He hasn't quit you yet, even with the things you have done to warrant it. That is something to rest well about at night.

Yes, you have a past you can't redo and things you would do differently. Do them differently moving forward. Do not let discouragement over your past keep you from God. One of Satan's main tactics is to get us to drown ourselves in shame so we will assume the worst about God and disqualify ourselves. See God knowing about your past not as an intrusion but as an *invitation*. It is the opportunity for you to love back the One person who has been the most faithful friend you have—a powerful space to welcome being fully known without fear.

When you enjoy God without hiding, you become unafraid of what anyone else thinks.

Because God knows about my past, my belief in His intention for my life can be restored.

Restore: 3 Steps to Move Forward

1. Find a quiet and private time to be alone with the Lord. Ask Him to bring to mind the things from your past you are struggling with that might even be showing up in other ways in your life. Pray about them, confess the ones that need confessing, and ask for forgiveness. Pray for healing for the ones done to you. Write them down in a journal or on a piece of paper. Then next to it write, "God knows about it. The blood of Jesus covered it." When you are finished, take a red marker and put an X over the whole paper to remind you these are things from your past. (Seek counseling for abuse/emotional trauma.)

2. Make a list of people from your past you find yourself wanting to make the past right with. Next to their names, write *approval* or *apology*, as you determine who you are simply wanting to gain approval from and who you truly owe an apology to. When apology is needed, make every effort to apologize—and then, move on.

3. Look back at the list of three practical boundary suggestions. Which of these most applies to an area you could use some work in? Choose one relationship or issue that needs a better boundary and make a plan for how to put that practical boundary suggestion into place within the next ten days.

07

God Knows Your Future

I am sure of this, that he who started a good work
in you will carry it on to completion.

Philippians 1:6 csb

Several months ago, the Lord brought to my attention something that had become a problematic nighttime ritual. For a few weeks, I had been lying in bed, quietly googling. A harmless activity in and of itself, but it had become consuming for me. So often this is the way the unsettling of my mind works; fear doesn't come in the front door but the back one. It is the subtleties of things like *checking on that . . . just doing my research* that often lead to a mental breaking down over time. Eventually, we wind up with a low hum of anxiety in the background of our thoughts, wearing us down subconsciously every day.

It wasn't necessarily the activity of googling that had

become an issue, since without Google, I am virtually lost in my own city when it comes to knowing everything from the best new place to get sushi to the phone number for my dog groomer (for the hundredth time). It was the frequency behind it. The way it had become a self-soothing activity to ease my worries about whatever I felt by asking more questions. And yes, the way it had replaced me going to God with my burdens at times too. Because after all, when you have Google answering your questions, you have fewer questions for the One who really knows.

Could Google really ease my concerns about the future? If you would have asked it to me like that, my eyebrow would have raised. I am, after all, a committed pragmatist. But maybe it could give me insight into my aches and pains. Maybe it could just let me know some type of heads-up to satisfy my need to plan things. Isn't that a good idea? Isn't that what everyone does, and isn't that harmless?

It would not be far-fetched to answer those questions with a yes. Most of us would not consider doing research a harmful activity. Except for when it *does* harm you, because you *still* don't know how your future is going to turn out, and that's really the question. You *still* don't feel better, safer, or more relieved, even though you've gone on a specific hunt for those treasures. And you *still* need just one more bit of reassurance that there is a way to prevent pain or problems for you and those you love. And you *still* don't turn to the actual Source of endless wisdom and help.

When we go to anything other than God as a replacement comfort for the unknowns of our future, we set ourselves back from quicker relief with the real thing.

We will always need *more*—more reassurance; to check one

more time. Always need to ask the question again. Always need more googling.

Google can't fix the fear you have over your future.

Google might have become your god, but it is not God.

This isn't really about Google. It's about our fear of a future that feels many times unstable and often unknown.

God knows if you're sick. He knows how the world ends. He knows where all the sinkholes in the world are. What might happen if we detoxed from our searching and decided to simply trust Him with all of it?

There comes a point when we must ask: Has my life improved from all the information I have gathered over the years?

Maybe it's given us a valuable piece of information for a stain-removal remedy. Perhaps it's made us aware of something that helped us feel better for a time. And certainly, important things like first-aid information, emergency numbers, and how to treat a snakebite or find a hotline number for help in crisis have been for many of us lifesaving tools. But no search engine can produce the type of security we need for a worried and questioning heart.

> When we go to anything other than God as a replacement comfort for the unknowns of our future, we set ourselves back from quicker relief with the real thing.

God's omniscience, however, covers it. His intimate knowledge of you is covering your future. He knew you from the beginning, and His presence in your life involves a thorough completion of the work you have to do on this earth—which He also knows all details about. So rest, because every bit of that timing will be exactly right.

The Questions We're Asking Versus
the Issues We're Really Having

Often, the question we ask isn't the true question.

When it comes to our future, what most of us really want to know, what keeps us up at night, is if we are going to be okay. But we don't ask that question, or at least we ask it in a roundabout way. The issue we are really having is not *lacking information*, even though we are on the constant knowledge hunt; it is *lacking certainty*—that the kind of future we, our kids, grandkids, and future generations are going to have, with all the world's unrest, will not be a complete disaster. Peel the onion down a little more and you will hit the core issue of trust. Because at the bottom of it all: if God doesn't know about our future, and if God's omniscience doesn't include provision for us amid the world's surrounding chaos, we are justified in our worry. If, though, we believe the opposite, we have no grounds for it.

There is a measurable cause for our worry, despite what we know. We live under a *conditions-based* mentality. This, in turn, drives the way we live our everyday lives. There is an important tie, here, to what I cover in my book *Jesus Over Everything*, about the preeminence of Christ, talked about in Colossians 1:17–18: "He is before all things, and by him all things hold together. He is also the head of the body, the church; he is the beginning, the firstborn from the dead, so that he might come to have first place in everything" (CSB). As I wrote in that book, there is a statement in Latin regarding worship: *Lex orandi, lex credendi, lex vivendi*—which means as we worship, so we believe, so we live.

When the conditions of our lives become what we hold in highest regard and, as a result, we spend our time focused on them and how they will affect our future, that means they are a part of the temporal system of this earth we are in the habit of worshiping. In other words, we worship our cars, our homes, our relationships, our looks, our media, our vacations, our food, and so on. We often put them above God. So it is no wonder that when it comes time to have conversation about the future, what we've been worshiping has put us on shifting sand. It has led us to mindsets and daily lifestyles (a.k.a. googling for information) that don't support the security we can and should have in Christ, because they are our primary focus and thus, unreliable anchors. And we know it. This leads us to staying in a constant state of worry. It is also quite revealing about what we've been worshiping, and why putting Jesus first is truly our first order of business to straighten out—because when we worship Him, our belief in His sovereignty in our lives naturally increases, and our lives show proof.

After we take care of that first-priority order of business, the remedy to spending our days in mental turmoil and stress will be moving away from a *conditions-based mentality* into a *certainty mentality*. With Jesus in His right and proper place, a new sense of certainty is a by-product. It is not a one-and-done but a daily practice to stay near to Jesus, and it is a practice that, if it is important enough to us, we will be eager to do. Those of us who speak of a constant weariness are mostly weary mentally. Our bodies might also be tired, but they are likely responding to the constant mental activity our minds are putting it through. Enough is enough. Believers in Jesus have the

> When we worship Him, our belief in His sovereignty in our lives naturally increases, and our lives show proof.

159

security of certainty. So living focused on our conditions is living below par.

Sometimes it's helpful to see our behaviors in black and white, so let's look at the main questions we are asking right now about the future and the real issues we are having, so we can know what's going on and know what we need to be addressing.

Questions We're Asking
- What is the future going to look like?
- Why doesn't God intervene in this evil culture?
- Does God see what's going on in this world and in my world?

(Some of us, too, are increasingly interested in the end times, which is wonderful, on one hand, since we should be interested in all of the Bible. But our questions about prophecy may also be more about wanting reassurance about the future than true interest in how the end of times affects the way we live today for the kingdom of God. Something to consider.)

Issues We're Really Having
- Struggling to trust God
- Battling to give up personal control
- Getting our priorities out of whack
- Looking to outside comfort

There may be other issues at play, but these are often primary. Our relationship with God is a process—it is not a perfect and painless journey in which we do not have our days of doubt and even, at times, feelings of despair. David loved God with all his heart, but the psalms he wrote often spoke of that despair he fought. It is not sinful to have feelings that contradict our faith. It is detrimental to us to allow those feelings to overtake it.

It may feel at times like we must go on what we see—that we must respond and react to our conditions and it is up to us to save ourselves by some type of human measure. We do this in so many ways—even methods that sneak up on us and become consuming, like googling; things that seem even positive like our organized planning; and things that we don't recognize as a method of our control at all, like prediction (stick around—I'm about to tell you a lot more about that). But trusting our limited knowledge *is* a trust in conditions. In this, we rely on the tools we have—the conditions we see, taste, feel, sense, touch, and can understand. The difference between us and God is that He actually *knows*. He doesn't rely on unreliable tools of measurement. He doesn't

> God handles our future best because His knowledge is based in certainty.

have feelings that interfere with facts. God handles our future best because His knowledge is based in *certainty*. And as we worship Him, we move from certainty in ourselves to certainty in Him.

Control

One big question we avoid asking is the one many of us are dealing with: *Is there a way I can control this?*

My friend Sharon Hodde Miller, in her book *The Cost of Control*, cites a podcast interview she heard with a church historian named Sarah Hinlicky Wilson who says something I also firmly believe to be true: *humans cannot tolerate uncertainty.*[1] This is, again, why Jesus is the answer the terrified world craves. Sharon goes on to write that, "When we look back on the history of the church, as well as the history of the world, we see humanity rebelling against the limitations of our own knowledge and control by claiming insight that God has not given us and asserting control we do not possess."[2]

Besides the fact we are in a constant battle with our own flesh, which wants equality with God, we like control because we know how to follow a process. We can obey rules. We can print out a template. We will eagerly pay for a course with a good strategy. We can't wait to get our hands on a new planner. We are good at making lists. If there is a way to control a future that feels uncontrollable, we will.

Our questions about the future might at times be simple curiosity, but most of the time they are more about determining our next move. Making plans is one thing; making plans in order to play God with our future is another. We will likely never admit it is the latter, but the mad scramble of control measures usually gives it away.

We know we are supposed to be believing God in this, so we don't like to expose ourselves for our micromanagement. We know that when we say we are worried for our future we expose that we lack trust in God. So instead we will say:

"I just don't know what kind of world my kids are going to grow up in."

"If it keeps going like this, I'm going to have to go live off the grid with my family."

> **Making plans is one thing; making plans in order to play God with our future is another.**

"Government is ruining our country. It's all up to us to turn it around."

These things may have some truth and possibly even some positive elements to them. First and foremost, our angst may drive us to our knees to pray. Christians aren't called to live passive—prayer is an action and so is putting feet to those prayers. But we *do* know what kind of world our kids are going to grow up in—a difficult and godless one. So we can stop being shocked. (Grieved, yes. But not shocked.) And living off the grid with our family sounds amazing, but how does that fit with the Matthew 28:19 call to go into all the world and make disciples? The government might be ruining our country since flawed human beings run it, but we are all ruining it because anyone other than God cannot help but in some way make a mess. Beyond the responsibility to vote and be active in advocating in political ways that will make a difference, since when is *anything* hinging on us alone?

Circling our own wagons for our own comfort and relief is not the answer. That's a form of control.

Disengaging from the hard things and hunkering down with our families is not the answer. That's a form of control.

Blaming everything wrong on poor leadership is not the answer. That's a form of control.

The answer lies in asking God to change us, even in a godless culture, to help us see Him, do right, and stay focused on living the gospel. Praying for an eternal perspective, even in the here and now. Keeping our eyes on Jesus. Prioritizing Christ, our future-holder. Being active in our lives and the lives of others, and living out of the call to follow Christ, not comfort or convenience. God's omniscience over everything that is and will happen to us allows us to rest, even in the unrest of our lives.

God's omniscience over everything that is and will happen to us allows us to rest, even in the unrest of our lives.

When God inspired these words thousands of years ago, "Do not let your hearts be troubled and do not be afraid" (John 14:27), He knew about today. He knew the world wasn't going to get easier. And yet He spoke these words for our future.

Our control gets in the way of that. It not only doesn't actually help control any of the things we think it does, but it creates the opposite: we become enslaved to its illusion. Our belief in its benefit to us (often subliminally) has convoluted our concept of the difference between due diligence and personal power, the latter of which drives us to need it more while being overcome by its destruction.

And there is something else. What we believe about God's authority is important here, because as we trust who He is over our humanity, we are less disillusioned about what our meager attempts at control can produce.

- God's authority knows no limits and is absolute.

    "The LORD has established his throne in heaven, and his kingdom rules over all." (Psalm 103:19 CSB)
- God's authority is in relationship to His righteousness and justice.

    "Righteousness and justice are the foundation of your throne; faithful love and truth go before you." (Psalm 89:14 CSB)
- God delegates authority to humanity for us to reflect the righteous and just rule of God on earth.

    "Doing what is righteous and just is more acceptable to the LORD than sacrifice." (Proverbs 21:3 CSB)

And in case you have forgotten, God's attributes absolutely affect your daily life. In getting to know more about Him, we develop confidence from that interconnectedness. We gain life skills and new levels of coping from learning from His example. This is why greater self-exploration isn't the true key to relief from worrying about our future. We already know we cannot fix the world's mess, so it only brings us more angst. And it only drives us to dig in and try to find new methods to control it, which leads to more exhaustion.

If control just came in the front door, we might be willing to call it like we see it. But that's just it: we don't always see it, or at least recognize it for what it is.

Sometimes it comes to us in the form of a habit, like my googling. It was not the only problematic habit I've formed in recent years.

Back in 2020, when things were going a bit haywire for all of us, every morning I would walk through my living room to the sound of my TV telling me what "might," "probably will," or "could" happen with the health pandemic we were experiencing in the world. Soon, it became my *hello* to every single morning—my new normal that eventually seeped into my bones like the deepest marrow of dread.

And I, a good soldier of lifelong planning and list-making, did what I knew to do with the information I was being told by the news: started creating mental scenarios of game plans *if it came to this* or *in the event* things went on however long. I sent my family articles about what experts were saying about all the ins and outs, ways to prepare, and what to believe. I learned to be a fantastic in-house reporter of future happenings, and with every support piece of information I gathered, I felt more and more confident.

Until, of course, some new major piece of information came out that was different. Then I would have to pivot. Sent scrambling for the latest, I found myself hoping but fearing my source could be wrong, that someone might know better, and the cycle would have to begin all over again. I lived in the privilege of being in the know and paid its steep price of mental ambiguity.

I watched it compromise the souls of my friends too. Some of them became increasingly isolated. Some of them, increasingly bitter. Some of them became different people altogether, no longer able to carry on conversations about any other kind of life but controversies, conspiracies, or fear. Some of them, to this day.

I saw what making plans based on conditions will do in real time: pull us from living in the reality of biblical certainties and cause us to focus on imaginations and projections—mirages that we are convinced look 100 percent real. Conditions that are real, but in the scheme of the promise of eternal security, are still *conditional.*

The most common way we make plans for a future we cannot control is to try to predict things. It is a way we know to compensate—self-soothe—when we feel the walls falling all around us. God spoke to me about that in the midst of my scrambling during those early days of the pandemic—it was something I got caught up in doing. But prediction is just another form of control. Isn't that something? All our due diligence can work wildly against us in the end. If we can try to predict what will happen next, we can feel some type of relief. We are willing, even, to take the temporary kind.

Prediction is just another form of control.

So, you see, whether it's stockpiling, or manically watching the news, or reading articles online, or googling ourselves to sleep, it's all different faces of the same issue.

Control is a fake relationship, but we still love it.

We keep thinking control serves us, but it doesn't. So don't be surprised, when you begin to make steps of progress in giving up control (look for some practical help with that at the end of the chapter), if you still miss its illusion. A lot of us are used to control, and the craving of that false sense of security doesn't die easily; it often lures us back.

We are clever with our means to gain control and will often try to regain some sense of it.

You wouldn't be the first to make some progress with giving up control only to eventually try to regain it. Again, it is a long-held practice for us that dies hard. We'd rather have physical control, but we will take mental when physically our hands are tied about something. (It's fascinating to watch us try to compensate!)

We have a double standard about God being in control.

We like the idea that God is in control for things that serve us, but not for things that don't. When it means evil doesn't win, we are on board with the idea. ("God, please take control of this situation and bring me justice!") But when it means things aren't going our way, we resist. ("I don't like the way you're handling this, God!") So we even try to control the issue of control, itself. We especially love to control how God exercises it in our lives.

For the last six months, I've heard friends, neighbors, and people all over the internet say over and over how very tired they are. I'm tired too. Trying to gain control has so much to do with it. God is the only One who knows the magnitude of the mysteries of our future, and He does not tire while maintaining perfect control.

Fear

When my daughter was little, she was on the road to becoming a terrific tumbler. I watched her attack all the gymnastics events with that look of determination on her young face. But one day she fell on her head while doing a back handspring. She never wanted to tumble again, and within three months, she quit gymnastics.

Our fears can stop us from greatness. They stop us from basic living too.

I've watched this pattern; something happens to people, and it kickstarts other things. I've seen people go from reasonable in their fear to paralyzed from it. Before you know it, it becomes not about the original issue anymore. Once fear gets its teeth into you, a lot of once-irrational things suddenly make sense.

I started calling this observation a "fear loop" a few years ago because it felt like a loop people couldn't get off that just kept going around and around—one thing bleeding into another, fear upon fear upon fear, in a never-ending cycle. And many of the fears were completely warranted. We watched people die from a largely unknown disease, often our family members. Many of us couldn't just turn a page on that because we were forever affected. It was (and continues to be) a brutal teacher. I learned the difference between honoring people and enabling paranoia. I learned what it meant to do my

> Our fears can stop us from greatness. They stop us from basic living too.

due diligence but keep believing God was ultimately in control. But there were nights, for me too, when it threatened to rival what I knew to be true about God.

All of us have fears over things; in many ways, this is natural. We don't get into loops simply because we experience fear. It is when we do not properly deal with our fear that we often get into these loops we cannot easily escape. In my observation and own personal experience, this is what I've seen:

Fear Loop

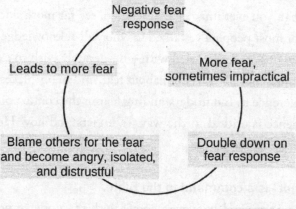

*Triggered by an improperly handled natural fear response.

Negative fear response

More fear, sometimes impractical

Double down on fear response

Blame others for the fear and become angry, isolated, and distrustful

Leads to more fear

copyright Lisa Whittle

When we get into a fear loop, these things typically happen:

- The thing we started out fearing usually grows, morphs, or changes into something else.
- We isolate because we feel like people see our fear as extreme and/or we are misunderstood.
- We try to minimize how afraid we are.
- We get frustrated when people don't accept our fear.
- We try to rationalize our fear as normal, justified, and right.
- Our fear eventually causes us to miss out on things we care about.

Our fears often start out valid. But then the loops occur. If you've ever been on an interstate that loops around a city you don't know your way around, you know what it feels like to be on a road you endlessly keep looping, and before you know it, you've seen every side of a city. This is the way it is with a fear loop. You'll spend far more time and energy on every fear that exists than you ever imagined or wanted, see far more sides to it, and—for most people I've talked to who will acknowledge this is something they've struggled with—desperately wish to exit off.

So much has been written about fear, and many places in the Bible reference it. But understanding fear in the context of God's omniscience is critical to the way we understand how He helps us when we experience it.

"Fear not" is a command in the Bible.

This command, however, comes with the understanding of our imperfect humanity. The command implies that there *is fear,* which suggests in our flesh it won't ever completely be eradicated. In other words, the issue isn't the absence of fear, but what we do with the fear when we experience it. God clearly knew and knows that we will experience fear. In His strength there is victory over our bouts with it.

The subject of fear in the Bible in relation to God is about awe, reverence, and holy trepidation.

It is intended to keep us from getting too casual with our almighty God. As the world's pull is to humanize God and remove Him from His holiness, He clearly knew and knows the importance of remaining set apart in a category all of His own.

There is a biblical correlation with us knowing more, and how it produces more fear and anxiety in us.

Again, this is not suggesting we stay uneducated or bury our heads in the sand. It is talking about the pursuit of knowing, in lieu of deferring our information and insights to God. Give this heavy consideration if you've been living overwhelmed and thinking watching the news will bring deep relief. It is proof, again, of why God's knowledge of all that is and will happen in the world and in your life is withheld from you—not out of cruelty, but out of love, since we cannot bear the mental anguish that comes with it. Remember the words of Solomon? "For with much wisdom comes much sorrow; the more knowledge, the more grief" (Ecclesiastes 1:18).

God is so good to us to protect us from what we could have no way of knowing . . . that, if we were to have the information we think we want, we likely could not bear it.

A New Mindset About the Future

For all our complaining about how God doesn't fill us in on His plans, we cannot claim that He has not been crystal clear from the beginning of time about His intent for our future. "Whoever finds his life will lose it, and whoever loses his life for my sake will find it" (Matthew 10:39 ESV). These were Jesus' commissioning words to His disciples, and they are the same words for us today.

Most of us, however, think about our future in terms of *preservation: What can I do to protect myself, keep myself and my loved ones safe, happy, and healthy, and live a long life here on earth?*

But God created life—and, as a result, our future—to be about *loss.*

In the plan of God, that *gift* of loss was a loving one, since He knows what incredible things await us. ("For to me, to live is Christ and to die is gain" [Philippians 1:21].) He wants us to make good use of our lives in the interim, but we find a greater benefit once we leave here. Yet we still crave the lesser life. It's a small example, but I imagine this to be like when my toddlers wanted to play in a cardboard box while much more expensive toys sat untouched in their playroom. The plight of humanity is constantly settling for the mediocre things because they seem fantastic to us in their proximity and familiarity, though they do not even compare to the things of God.

Accepting loss as God's intention for our future might be more palatable if loss didn't involve people, and people weren't our deepest loves. Especially in the early weight of it, loss cannot possibly feel like a gift. We simply do not know how to be willing to consider this.

It is only because anything is possible with the help of God ("I can do all things through Christ who strengthens me" [Philippians 4:13 NKJV]) that a future with the intent of loss-for-gain can become appealing. It is a mindset only He can produce in us, as we allow Him to move us from the one of surplus and preservation we are fixated on.

Because we live within the limited experience of how life here is wonderful, our attachment to it is understandable. And it's confusing, because sometimes, it is wonderful. God makes it beautiful, because life on earth, though hard, is also a gift—families, laughter, sunsets, flowers, breezes, oceans, food, church, coffee, mountains, smiles, hugs, Krispy Kreme doughnuts. It is just that the gift of life on earth is incomparable to the gift of heaven. But because we haven't experienced what is to come for us, and because we do not know what God does, it will require us taking His word for it. We cannot make the shift without trust.

> The plight of humanity is constantly settling for the mediocre things because they seem fantastic to us in their proximity and familiarity, though they do not even compare to the things of God.

As we cling to the life we know and love, our inability to get peace over our future comes from the constant pain of the tight grip. It serves as a reminder that not quite everything was on the table when we committed our lives to God. Life, itself, has to be on the table. When you try to hold onto something that was created with an intention to be let go, it will cause you pain.

This is an aspect of God's sovereignty that is difficult for us, but it can be freeing. If we are hungry to be more settled about our future and open to allowing God to settle us, this mindset shift can not only create that needed dependency on Christ and trust for His ultimate wisdom, but also free us from having to scramble to hold on to something we are losing anyway. I recently interviewed a dear woman named Colleen who is dying of stage-four cancer and who openly talked about what it feels like to be honest about how loss is her destiny. "Loss is *all* of our futures," I say to her on my podcast, *Jesus Over Everything*, because the truth is, we are all dying every day. No one loves to read that, but what if its reality could beautifully set us free from pretending we live forever on this earth? What if instead of shying away from the conversation, we faced it? Could it help us stop our exhausting methods of forcing our lives to stay preserved? Maybe we would weep over hard health diagnoses less. Maybe it would let us embrace aging without forcing our skin to stay young. And maybe the pressure could be off to hold on so tightly to ourselves—and those we love most. It's a beautiful privilege to be alive. And it's an even more beautiful privilege to get to see Jesus.

We are all nearing our future more and more every day. This is good news, believers.

God created you with your end in mind. In fact, it is your end He is the *most* interested in. The end is the beginning of the new creation. He has our reunion on His mind.

King Solomon put this blunt spin on the realities of humanity: "He has made everything beautiful in its time. He has also set eternity in the human heart; yet no one can fathom what God has done from beginning to end" (Ecclesiastes 3:11).

Solomon was right. We crave eternity because Christ put it in our hearts to long for it. But we do not have His mind. So we wrestle in the great in-between.

The gift of life

on earth is

incomparable to

the gift of heaven.

The gift of li

on earth is

incomparabl

the gift of h

A Firm Foundation

I woke up not long ago with a hymn on my mind:

> *How firm a foundation, ye saints of the Lord,*
> *is laid for your faith in God's excellent Word!*
> *What more can be said than to you God hath said,*
> *to you who for refuge to Jesus have fled?*[3]

As soon as I got my morning coffee, I began to research it, knowing by now that things like this don't just *randomly* come up. I found nothing about this old hymn from 1787 that particularly stood out, except there isn't much to know about it. I could only conclude that the significance of it coming to mind wasn't in its history but the words of the song itself.

For days prior, I had been concerned for my kids and the world they were going to raise families in. Though they are themselves now grown, a mother never stops being concerned. It hits me now and then, often in the night, that I cannot manage their lives for them. If the circle of life works right, I will be gone first. And I don't like that I will not be here to help them, even though they don't rely on me in that way anymore.

Their foundation is firm, Lisa. I am the firm foundation. I sensed God speak to my heart. The comfort in those words felt preciously overwhelming.

The reality for all of us is often a scary one. It is often confusing, complicated, and fills us with fear. But that's just temporary. Those are true feelings, but it's also true that God is the ground on which we stand. And often in the worries for our future, He is taking us somewhere we simply cannot see yet.

I don't know if you know the story about Hezekiah, but if there was anyone who couldn't see what God was doing, it was he. If anyone's future looked bleak, it was his. You don't have much hope for your future when God tells you that you're going to die.

> In those days Hezekiah became ill and was at the point of death. The prophet Isaiah son of Amoz went to him and said, "This is what the LORD says: Put your house in order, because you are going to die; you will not recover." Hezekiah turned his face to the wall and prayed to the LORD, "Remember, Lord, how I have walked before you faithfully and with wholehearted devotion and have done what is good in your eyes." And Hezekiah wept bitterly. (2 Kings 20:1–3)

I would weep bitterly too if I got that word from the Lord. Proof, again, that God's voice to us often comes through process of elimination—Hezekiah would have undoubtedly given himself better news, so he had to know this was God's voice and not his.

This interchange with Hezekiah and God has always moved me. I like it because it's real. It's not a polished, edited version. It reminds me of the rawness I've lived at times with God over difficult moments in my life, weeping so hard my eyes were red and swollen.

There's a lot more to the story of Hezekiah. One such thing worth noting: according to Scripture, he was special, beyond his role of king. "Hezekiah trusted in the LORD, the God of Israel. There was no one like him among all the kings of Judah, either before him or after him" (2 Kings 18:5). Hezekiah's relationship with God undoubtedly created a bond of trust between himself and God, but also a confidence in Hezekiah to petition Him in prayer, asking for more time to be added to his life. And God was moved by his prayers.

> Before Isaiah had left the middle court, the word of the LORD came to him: "Go back and tell Hezekiah, the ruler of my people, 'This is what the LORD, the God of your father David, says: I have heard your prayer and seen your tears; I will heal you. On the third day from now you will go up to the temple of the LORD. I will add fifteen years to your life. And I will deliver you and this city from the hand of the king of Assyria. I will defend this city for my sake and for the sake of my servant David.'" (2 Kings 20:4–6)

In the event you have gone down the road of becoming a skeptic, doubtful that God is willing to alter His hand or change His mind, please consider God's response to Hezekiah's tears and prayers. We don't know exactly why God changed course on extending Hezekiah's life. But the suggestion here is that the actions of Hezekiah helped facilitate it. This alone should give us proof if we ever begin to question how much prayers matter; they are, indeed, an act of spiritual activism. Not one is a waste. People who live faithfully to God don't live different futures than unfaithful people in many of their circumstances alone. They live different futures because they, themselves, are different in the way they approach them. Much of that happens in a prayer life.

There is at least one caveat to this beautiful story.

God does extend Hezekiah's life by fifteen years, but it doesn't come without ramification.

In the extension of his life and in his prosperity, Hezekiah develops a sense of pride. It is not completely clear but suggested through Scripture that either as a result of those blessings or because of the request, itself, while it benefits Hezekiah, it results in hardship for future generations.

> Then Isaiah said to Hezekiah, "Hear the word of the LORD: 'Look, the days are coming when everything in your palace and all that your predecessors have stored up until today will be carried off to Babylon; nothing will be left,' says the LORD. 'Some of your descendants—who come from you, whom you father—will be taken away, and they will become eunuchs in the palace of the king of Babylon.'" Then Hezekiah said to Isaiah, "The word of the LORD that you have spoken is good," for he thought, "Why not, if there will be peace and security during my lifetime?" (2 Kings 20:16–19)

When Hezekiah made the request for extra years, he did so with a human thought process and not with the omniscience of God. He didn't know and couldn't see the entire picture. Could God have denied it? Yes. We don't know exactly why He did not. But the importance here is that even good people want what best serves us. We never know exactly what we are asking from a full-picture perspective, even when prayer requests seem best to us. Sometimes our human requests are shortsighted.

None of us is completely unselfish in asks for our future. Great people have thought we've known better than God. We might be expert planners, but we are not sovereign.

> Great people have thought we've known better than God. We might be expert planners, but we are not sovereign.

Because this is true, we cannot completely trust our desires and asks—we can only trust God's. Only His ways are without flaw or bias.

Our futures are powerfully and tenderly given oversight by God. Powerfully, in the sense He has all knowledge, wisdom, and dominion over them. Tenderly, in the sense that everything that happens to us is based in lovingkindness. This is why we can rest knowing our futures are in His hands.

- **Only God knows what your future holds.** We will never be able to know, even when we think we know—even when we plan it to the very best of our abilities.
- **Your future is intended for the purpose that you will live to praise and honor God.** Living for ourselves isn't the plan.
- **Only God has the power of life and death for you and your family.** We can do things to not hinder or hurt our life, but we don't truly control anything.
- **Your prayers and tears of concern for the future are seen and heard by God.** This *is* what you wonder about, right? If God sees and hears you?

Not only does God see and hear you, but He is taking you somewhere—through the pain, confusion, hardship, and fear for tomorrow.

He's taking you closer to His heart. *What a prize.*

Because at His heart is comfort. At His heart is peace. At His heart is relief. At His heart is joy, despite. At His heart are strength and hope.

The point of any hardship isn't for us to wise up about life. It is for us to willingly give up more and more of it.

Despite the aspects of difficulty in Hezekiah's story, we cannot miss the most important part: not the prolonged years but the depth of relationship that undoubtedly developed between Hezekiah and God as God brought him closer to His heart through the hardship of facing death. Even for the future generations that subsequent hardship came upon . . . even for us, today, as we go through tough days and painful experiences . . . the process of drawing nearer to God is what matters the most throughout it.

What if God has been wanting to take you somewhere you haven't been able to see because you have been too busy worrying about the future?

What if He has been bringing you in, inch by inch, sometimes with you resisting, to His very heart so that you would be able to find the strength you so desperately need to endure?

What if the answer you have been seeking isn't another avenue to find peace in your life but the spiritual activism of prayer? Much more about developing muscle in you than doing something that helps feed your need to control things?

The point of Hezekiah's life wasn't ever about the outcome. It was about the relationship. That is the point of your life too.

Trust Jesus with your future. No matter what. As C. S. Lewis wrote in his famous book *The Screwtape Letters*: "[The Enemy's] cause is never more in danger than when a human, no longer desiring, but still intending . . . looks round upon a universe from which every trace of [God] seems to have vanished, and asks why he has been forsaken, and

> The point of any hardship isn't for us to wise up about life. It is for us to willingly give up more and more of it.

181

still obeys."[4] I know God sometimes seems absent from this world. But in these times believers need to become very used to the words, "I trust You, still."

Know that in the space of the now and not yet, there will be weariness and groaning. Expect it. This is natural. Take it to God with prayer and, if you're like me, often, tears.

Praise Him for the glorious future that is ahead. What a good plan He has for us. Don't fear it or try to control it.

And get yourself ready.

Because God knows about the future, I can rest.

Rest: 3 Steps to Move Forward

1. Practice taking every negative thought captive, as in 2 Corinthians 10:5: "We take every thought captive to obey Christ" (csb). As a thought comes into your mind that is worrisome about your future, make your mind think of something else by having a list of ten beautiful things you love, are thankful for, or are promises that are true from Scripture that you can go to in that moment. (Have them on a sticky note in several places you need them—in your purse, in the car, in the kitchen, your bathroom, etc. Say it out loud!)

2. Study one story of God's power per month over the next six months. During the thirty days you study that one story, write down these things: what God

did, how things looked before His intervention, and why humans weren't capable of doing the job. Make any other notes about it to remind you of why He is the One who is worthy to be in charge of your life instead of you. The best way for us to defer control to God is not merely behavior modification. It is heart change. As we grow in our trust of God, we desire to give Him greater control of our lives. Some suggested power stories to study: Joshua 10; Mark 5; Acts 3–4; Ezekiel 37; 1 Kings 19.

3. Write down three questions you find yourself asking a lot about the future. Then next to them write down the issue you are really having (hint: look back at the list in the chapter to see if any of these apply). Pray over each issue.

God Knows What You Need to Release

I lift up my eyes to the mountains—where does my help come from?
My help comes from the LORD, the Maker of heaven and earth.

Psalm 121:1–2

We stood as a group of thirteen, with no thoughts of luck on our minds—just yieldedness to the Holy Spirit. He had been working inside our hearts all weekend at Levi Oaks, my newly renovated barn turned ministry space, which just nine months prior had been full of cobwebs, walls of ant families, and stray rusty nails. This was my first gathering there with my ministry team.

We all held different colors of balloons in our hands, a beautiful reminder of the kaleidoscope of our own lives, stories, struggles, and hopes. Tucked inside them were words we had written on white scraps of paper—what we needed to release to God.

As if on cue, the sky started misting, representing our soul's tears.

I knew from the time I started writing this book I wanted to physically enact what I had been dreaming about, writing about, living—things I, myself, needed to release to God. There is nothing special about the sky or a balloon release, but there is something about tangibles. Stakes in the ground. Stones of remembrance. Symbolism can help solidify things happening inside.

I led us outside, each of us holding our balloons like treasures, taking turns making small talk and looking up at the sky. After a few minutes, it got holy quiet. I don't remember, but I think I may have said a small prayer.

And then, on three, we let them go.

Up they went—all the beautiful colors carrying our burdens—lifted into the mouth of the blue sky, where kids imagine Jesus' mansion. Smaller and smaller they became, until they were specks against a cloudy haze.

The sky wouldn't solve our problems.

The balloon release wasn't the answer to the burdens, worries, and whys.

But it felt good to remember that God was.

And now, here *we* are.

We've talked about dreams and injustices, limitations, secret struggles, pain, and the past. We've looked at our futures and been honest about needing relief from our worries and whys. We've discussed fear loops and new coping methods for justice seeking. We've talked boundaries, biases, and the more profound experiences of life.

What will you do with all of it?

Lift Your Eyes

Around fifty-two times it tells us in Scripture to lift our eyes. *Fifty-two.*[1]

I suspect God knew it would be our natural posture in this difficult life, with broken dreams and burdened hearts, to look down instead of looking up.

The beautiful psalm of Ascent, Psalm 121, is perhaps the most famous for its encouragement to us to lift our eyes. "I look up to the mountains; does my strength come from mountains? No, my strength comes from GOD" (Psalm 121:1–2 MSG). But the interesting context is that like so much of Scripture, it's much more a realignment from our distractions and misplacements than a sweeping, cinematic love note. My friend, theologian Dr. Joel Muddamalle, explains it like this:

> In Psalm 121 the Psalmist says he, "lifts his eyes to the hills" and wonders if his help will come from there. At first, as we read this; we may think that looking to the hills is a good thing, but the psalmist is actually warning us. Often, through Scripture we are told to lift our eyes to the heavens and in doing so be reminded of the greatness and grandeur of God.
>
> In the ancient world the altars of the gods of the pagans were placed on hills and mountain tops. The ancient people believed these hills and mountains were the places where the

gods lived. So, when the Psalmist questions if help will come from the hills it is a subtle rebuke of the false gods of the nations. It is also a warning for the people of God not to be lured into the false promises of security, stability, and salvation that the fake gods present.[2]

Maybe you've never before considered the logistics of this. But there is a crucial space between looking down and looking up where the danger of distraction lies. In that space, where hundreds of distractions present themselves, it threatens to pull us away from looking to God, our True Help. That small space. Such a little detail. And yet it is in those in-between places— where we haven't quite lifted our eyes all the way to God and settled for momentary comforts—that He feels far, silent, and out of touch with our lives.

Where are we looking for God?

How have our eyes gotten distracted in finding Him?

What do we need to release to His care?

The more we resist what we need to release, the more we refuse our own pain relief.

My friend, I know you have been through the wringer. I know that life has been enormously hard on you and it's hard not to focus on your circumstances. I know you may not feel like lifting your eyes to God. Maybe you feel He isn't handling things because so far your life says He hasn't handled them—at least not in the way you prefer. But what if you just don't know? What if you can't see because you are looking down instead of up?

The lifting of the eyes command in

> The more we resist what we need to release, the more we refuse our own pain relief.

Scripture had everything to do with the true awareness of who humans were in light of who God was and is. It was never about us. It is never about us. This is why we explore the omniscience of God. This alone gives us relief from the pressure and self-expectation and internal drive to take on responsibilities that were never ours. Aren't we tired of our temporary solutions?

You don't need a balloon release to give your worries over to God. You can pray this very simply: *God, I release _____ to You. I can't hold on to it anymore.*

And if you aren't even there yet, here's an alternative: *God, I want to release _____ to You. I can't hold on to it anymore. Help get me there.*

These prayers might seem simple.

But many times, pausing even a minute from our compulsive fixing allows us to in some way begin to see God.

Easy Versus Beautiful

Lisa of 1990, wild and wandering, would have never dreamed of what God knew her life would look like in thirty years. I bet your life isn't the way you planned, either—in some way, at least.

We don't know what we don't know about what God wants to do in our lives and futures, and sometimes, because we are so focused on trying to figure those things out ourselves, we miss the beauty of how He is loving us in the regular moments of our lives, even today.

Our lives aren't easy, but there's a difference between easy and beautiful. God knows us so well. And He knows the best places to love us.

How is God loving you these days? How is your not-easy life still beautiful?

We often look for the big ways for God to show up in our lives, but we miss the small ways He is showing up. Sometimes we don't see God loving us or feel God loving us in these ways because we are distracted. Sometimes we are overworked. Sometimes we are self-focused, overly critical, or bitter. Often we don't *know* God is loving us because we don't *notice*. The fact is, He knows your heart currency and customizes things in your life accordingly. How incredible is that? The fact that He is making something beautiful out of your life even though it's not easy?

Only God.

Your God Knows

I hope, wherever you are, this book has taken you closer to your God who knows.

Because if you come closer to Him, you will trust Him more. And that will help you release some things to Him, even today, which will help you feel His love for you.

That's all this life is, ultimately, you know: Jesus and you in the end. The rest is just holding on to Him while you get there.

> That's all this life is, ultimately, you know: Jesus and you in the end.

Five years ago, I wrote down what might happen if I understood and believed in the omniscience of God. Here is what I wrote, in no particular order.

If I really believe God knows . . .

- I won't waste so much mental energy on injustices I can't make right.
- I won't question God endlessly about things I'll never get answers to.
- I won't be angry so often.
- I won't keep so many secrets.
- I won't overexplain or overapologize to people so much.
- I will live more of my hopes and dreams without fear they won't come true.
- I will be less afraid of the pain I keep inside.
- I will stop trying to control every aspect of my life.
- I will not keep looking for relief in all the wrong places.
- I will stop trying to redo my past.
- I will feel more peace about my future.

I know what you may be thinking: *Can resting in the omniscience of God really do all that?* I realize it sounds lofty. But God *is* big enough. All of these things are by-products of living with the security of fully believing and trusting Him. Leaving our worries and whys with Him is our only true release and permanent relief and comfort.

Life for all of us is difficult, disappointing, and, in many regards, uncertain. But trust me when I tell you that there is so much we simply cannot know or see. Oh, you think you know everything about what's going on in your life? Not even close, my friend. Only God truly knows where you're going.

For so much of my life, I've just wanted God to do what

> **Oh, you think you know everything about what's going on in your life? Not even close, my friend. Only God truly knows where you're going.**

I want. But I've come to realize the parent who really loves you is not the one who fixes things for you. It's the one who says, "I can fix it for you, but I won't." Because that's the parent who knows true comfort and relief are found in the growth. Sometimes God has fixed things for me. And the times He hasn't? He's in some way mended my heart. He's always offered me *Himself*.

I've learned not to underestimate God's powerful hand in His quiet and still presence. Just because we cannot see or understand does not mean things aren't being done. One day, it will all be done. Only God knows when. Until then, He will not cease to meet us in our needs.

> **Just because we cannot see or understand does not mean things aren't being done.**

God is not far, unaware, unfeeling. Every pain, every dream, every injustice, every longing, every secret, every question, and every worry is on His mind.

You, my friend, will never leave His mind.

Finish Here

I gave my daughter, Shae, a bracelet not long ago that means a great deal to both of us, with the words on it, *Just breathe.* She wears it nearly every day.

Sometimes when she was little, in her worries, she was so panicked I could sense she was holding her breath and needed to exhale. I would tell her, "Honey, just breathe."

Shae also has asthma. The doctor said she might outgrow it, but it remains, and now it's been years. We've had some scares with her condition, so the phrase *Just breathe* comes with an even deeper level of meaning—and trust.

And when she went off to college, thousands of miles away from me, I could at times hear the worry in her voice and I would say to her over the phone to *just breathe*, like I did when she was young. And in my own set of worries, I would need to *just breathe* too, with my best friend so far away.

The *rûaḥ* of God is what sustained her those times—when

she couldn't breathe and when she chose to hold her breath. He knew her and knows her still. When I'm especially worried and missing her, Jesus comforts me with this knowledge.

The *rûaḥ* of God sustains you too. When you are holding your breath because it's hard and it hurts. And when you have the breath knocked out of you. He knew you and knows you still. It is not your will, your wit, you worrying hard enough. You became a living soul because He breathed into you. He wanted you. You weren't born in a hospital or with a doula—you were born by Him.

He knows *you.*

Release your burdens to Him.

Release your life to His care.

Look up. Lift your eyes.

Your God knows.

Notes

Introduction

1. Derek Kidner, *Genesis: An Introduction and Commentary*, vol. 1, Tyndale Old Testament Commentaries (Downers Grove, IL: InterVarsity Press, 1967), 3.

Chapter 1

1. Walter A. Elwell and Barry J. Beitzel, "Omniscience," in *Baker Encyclopedia of the Bible* (Grand Rapids, MI: Baker Book House, 1988), 1588.
2. Steven Tuell, "Nahum, Book of," ed. John D. Barry et al., *The Lexham Bible Dictionary* (Bellingham, WA: Lexham Press, 2016).

Chapter 2

1. Douglas Mangum et al., eds., *Lexham Theological Wordbook*, Lexham Bible Reference Series (Bellingham, WA: Lexham Press, 2014).
2. Lexico, s.v. "dream," https://www.dictionary.com/browse/dream.
3. https://www.crosswalk.com/faith/spiritual-life/does-god-still -give-prophetic-dreams.html.

4. Joel B. Carini, "God's Immutability," in *Lexham Survey of Theology*, ed. Mark Ward et al. (Bellingham, WA: Lexham Press, 2018).

5. Rick Warren, "What the Bible Says about the Doors in Your Life," Biblical Leadership (April 26, 2021).

6. Benjamin Reno Downer, James Orr, gen. ed., "Door," *International Standard Bible Encyclopedia* (1915), https://www.biblestudytools.com/dictionary/door/.

7. Lexico, s.v. "goal," https://www.dictionary.com/browse/goal.

Chapter 3

1. https://www.britannica.com/topic/Book-of-Isaiah.

Interstitial

1. Murray J. Harris, "The Second Epistle to the Corinthians: A Commentary on the Greek Text," *New International Greek Testament Commentary* (Grand Rapids, MI; Milton Keynes, UK: W.B. Eerdmans Pub. Co.; Paternoster Press, 2005), 445–49.

2. Diane Langberg, *Redeeming Power: Understanding Authority and Abuse in the Church* (Grand Rapids, MI: Brazos Press, 2020), 127.

Chapter 4

1. K. J. Ramsey, *This Too Shall Last: Finding Grace When Suffering Lingers* (Grand Rapids, MI: Zondervan, 2020), 54.

2. A. W. Tozer, *Man: The Dwelling Place of God* (Chicago: Moody Publishers), 5.

3. Donald A. Hagner, "Matthew 14–28," *Word Biblical Commentary* vol. 33B (Dallas: Word, Incorporated, 1995), 797.

Chapter 5

1. Amy Kenny, *My Body Is Not a Prayer Request* (Grand Rapids, MI: Brazos, 2022), 4.

2. Helen Keller, *Light in My Darkness* (London: Chrysalis Books, 2000).

3. Madeleine L'Engle, *Walking on Water: Reflections on Faith and Art* (Colorado Springs, CO: Convergent Books, 2016), 67.

Chapter 6

1. Maya Angelou, *The Poetry of Maya Angelou* (New York: Quality Paperback Book Club, 1993).

Chapter 7

1. Sharon Hodde Miller, *The Cost of Control* (Grand Rapids, MI: Baker, 2022), 27.
2. Miller, *The Cost of Control*.
3. John Rippon, publisher, "How Firm a Foundation," 1787 (public domain).
4. C. S. Lewis, *The Screwtape Letters* (New York: Touchstone, 1996 edition), 42.

Chapter 8

1. This search was done in Logos Bible Software in the ESV Bible Translation. Search results can vary based on Bible translation.
2. Joel Muddamallo, Instagram post, Scripture Walk Through IG: Psalm 121: The unexpected danger of "lifting your eyes," January 21, 2022, https://www.instagram.com/reel/CZPSewyheW1/?igshid=YmMyMTA2M2Y%3D.

Acknowledgments

To Scotty: you remain the biggest *God knows* of my life. Thank you to your handsome gray hair, which as you know I've been waiting for years to come in and also symbolizes the fact we are still here, better than ever.

To Graham, Micah, Shae, and Caroline: laughing with you is my favorite. Thank you for having your heads on straight and hanging out with Dad and me even when we are annoying.

To Mom: you are the great love of my life. Thank you for a hundred things words can't describe, and for your presence in my life, which has been the most consistent thing I know.

To Colleen: cue the song from *Beaches*. What we have isn't normal, and I know that. Thank you for twenty-eight years of "What are you doing today?" conversations.

To Lisa: thank you for being a boss, for getting me, for the belief that helps me soar.

To Damon, Stephanie, Lauren, and the great team at W: thank you for pursuing excellence on this and every project with me. A special thanks to Stephanie for matching my ridiculously high work-hours count on this one.

To Dr. Joel Muddamalle: thank you for enduring a first really bad batch of coffee and for coming back to help theologically inform on this book. It was fun nerding out with you, and your commitment to the Word made this book (and me) better.

To my LW team: thank you for killing it, keeping up with my brain, and being faithful servants of Jesus Christ. Thank you for never judging me for showing up with unwashed hair on basically every Zoom call.

To the readers: you're always on my mind. I fight to keep doing this because you invest in these pages. I write to honor Jesus and then, for you. I'll never take you for granted.

To my God, the One and Only Savior: thank You for allowing me the breath to do one more. Whatever else You have for me, I'm in.

About the Author

Lisa Whittle is the author of nine books and several Bible studies, including *Jesus Over Everything* and *The Hard Good*. She is a sought-out Bible teacher for her wit and bold, bottom-line approach. She is the founder of two online communities: Ministry Strong for ministry leaders and Called Creatives for writers and speakers, and host of the popular *Jesus Over Everything* podcast. She's a wife; mom; lover of laughter, good food, and the Bible; and a self-professed feisty work in progress.

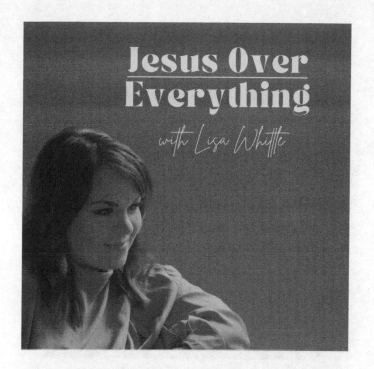

Jesus Over Everything

with Lisa Whittle

Jesus Over Everything with Lisa Whittle is a weekly podcast where best-selling author and speaker Lisa Whittle brings encouragement, Bible teaching, Christian living practical how-tos, and guest interviews for the listener on the go.

Every show is grounded in Lisa's signature relatable, bottom-line style with her passion to hold Jesus above everything.

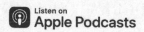

CALLED CREATIVES

God is doing *BIG* things in the hearts of women.

IT'S TIME TO ANSWER YOUR CALLING.

Led by best-selling authors, speakers, and industry experts, Lisa Whittle and Alli Worthington, Called Creatives is a private coaching community with hands-on training for writing and speaking with influence and impact.

GO DEEPER

WITH THE *YOUR GOD KNOWS* SIX-WEEK BIBLE STUDY WITH STREAMING VIDEO ACCESS

This unique, interactive video-based study and companion to *God Knows* immerses you in the truth of God's promises so you can know deep in your soul that a sovereign God understands your pain—and will one day make all things well.

Lisa Whittle draws on Scripture throughout the Old and New Testaments as she helps answer six critical questions for our times:

- Am I forgotten?
- How does good come from bad?
- Do my desires and dreams matter?
- Am I doomed by the sins of my family?
- Will God make wrong things right?
- Will I be okay?

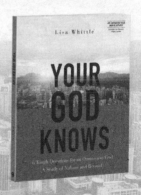